Flirting, Fun &
Chaotic Kisses

von Irene Zimmermann

PONS GmbH
Stuttgart

PONS

Flirting, Fun & Chaotic Kisses

von Irene Zimmermann
Englisch von Brian Melican

basierend auf den Geschichten „Küsse, Chaos, Fußballträume" und „Küsse, Chaos, Schlittenfahrt" von Irene Zimmermann aus den Büchern:

„Liebe, Schuss, Elfmeterkuss" © 2010
„Schneeflöckchen, Kuss & Kerzenschein" © 2007
by Planet Girl (Thienemann Verlag GmbH) Stuttgart/Wien

Auflage A1 5 4 3 2 / 2015 2014 2013 2012

© PONS GmbH, Rotebühlstraße 77, 70178 Stuttgart, 2010
PONS Produktinfos und Shop: www.pons.de
PONS Sprachenportal: www.pons.eu
E-Mail: info@pons.de

Englische Überarbeitung, Annotationen und Übungen: Brian Melican
Redaktion: Canan Özdamar
Logoentwurf: Erwin Poell, Heidelberg
Logoüberarbeitung: Sabine Redlin, Ludwigsburg
Einbandillustration: Birgit Schössow
Einbandgestaltung: Daniel Müller, Stuttgart
Sprecherin/Tonaufnahmen: Nicola Barber, New York
Layout: one pm, Petra Michel, Stuttgart
Satz: Digraf.pl - dtp services
Druck und Bindung: Print Consult GmbH, München

Printed in EU.
ISBN: 978-3-12-010021-8

INHALTSANGABE

Kisses, Chaos and Dreams of Football

Ein ganz normaler Samstagmorgen bei ihrer Freundin Mia ... und noch ahnt Natalie nichts Böses. Doch Mia hält eine schlimme Überraschung für sie bereit: 12 Sekunden kinoreifes Knutschen - festgehalten auf Mias Handy! Und die Hauptakteure sind Natalies Freund Felix und die coole Vanessa. Wie soll man da reagieren? Felix darauf ansprechen? Gleich Schluss machen? Oder vielleicht lieber eine ganze Nummer klüger handeln und sich über Vanessa bei Felix rächen? Soll Felix doch merken, wie es sich anfühlt, wenn man von einem Tag auf den anderen ausgetauscht wird! Da braucht Natalie nur noch einen anderen Jungen, der sich für Vanessa interessieren könnte: Mit diesen Gedanken im Kopf trifft sie auf ihren Klassenkameraden Leo...

Kisses, Chaos and Rides on a Sledge

Wer eine Zwillingsschwester hat, der weiß schon, wie nützlich das manchmal sein kann. Hanna ist todkrank - und das, wo doch am nächsten Tag der Wintersporttag stattfindet. Mit ihrem Bewunderer Maik und ohne sie !? Diese Gelegenheit darf auf gar keinen Fall verpasst werden! Wozu hat man eine Zwillingsschwester, denkt sich Hanna. Marie müsste nichts anderes tun, als einen Tag lang nicht von Maiks Seite zu weichen. Doch darauf hat Marie ganz und gar keine Lust ... bis sie erfährt, das ihr eigener Schwarm Andy auch dabei sein wird. Nur gibt es ein Problem: Hanna und Marie besuchen nicht die gleiche Schule und Marie hat nicht die geringste Ahnung, wie Hannas Freunde aussehen ...

AUFTRETENDE PERSONEN

Kisses, Chaos and Dreams of Football

Natalie

Natalie liebt das schnelle Leben und denkt nur ungern lange nach. Das hat Vorteile: Sie kommt schnell über Sachen hinweg und hat immer Freunde und Bekannte um sich. Der große Nachteil: Oft übersieht sie das, was auf der Hand liegt.

Mia

Mia denkt für sich selbst und für ihre beste Freundin Natalie mit: Manchmal nervt sie zwar mit ihren Beobachtungen und Bemerkungen, aber sie liegt mit ihnen selten ganz falsch.

Felix

Felix ist ein Mädchenschwarm und das weiß er auch. Deshalb tauscht er seine Freundinnen auch gerne einmal aus ... Dass er die Mädchen aber zuerst darüber in Kenntnis setzen sollte, dass die Beziehung vorbei ist, sieht er nur bedingt ein.

Leo

Leo ist ein ganz anderer Typ als Felix - ernsthaft und eher ein bisschen schüchtern. Unterschätzen sollte man ihn aber nicht: er weiß genau, wenn Mädchen ihn gut finden ... und er hat tolle grüne Augen.

Kisses, Chaos and Rides on a Sledge

Hanna & Marie

Die beiden sind Zwillingsschwestern, wie sie im Buche stehen - immer
füreinander da, aber jede mit ihren Eigenarten. Mit zwei Minuten ist Marie
die ältere und ernsthaftere von beiden - und nach Ansicht der flippigen
Hanna, die gerne das Leben ihrer Schwester mitorganisiert, hoffnungslos
unromantisch.

Andy

... ist Maries Schwarm - allerdings nicht nur ihrer. Während es zuerst so
aussieht, als ob Andy sich ernsthaft für Marie interessiert, merkt sie bald,
dass Andy ganz anders ist, als er scheint.

„Maik"

Maik ist höflich, nett und ein bisschen
schüchtern. Eigentlich so gar nicht
Hannas Typ - und eigentlich sehr schade,
dass er auf ihre Schwester steht.

Wie es sich für bes-
te Freundinnen und
Zwillingsschwestern
gehört, halten sich
sowohl Natalie & Mia
als auch Hanna &
Marie stets auf dem
Laufenden - natürlich
per SMS.

Daher findest Du an
einigen Stellen im
Text den einen oder
anderen „Hilferuf"
den eine von beiden
der anderen durch-
schickt.

Dabei gilt es brennen-
de „Love-Questions"
zu klären: Wer?
Wo? Und vor allem,
mit wem?

Beantworte die Fra-
gen. Eine Liste mit
SMS-Abkürzungen fin-
dest du auf S. 84 und
die Lösungen ab S.
123.

Irene Zimmermann

Kisses, Chaos
and Dreams of Football

TR. 01 "Now, you have to be very, very brave[1]," whispers[2] Mia, my friend, in my ear as she pulls me away from the paddling pool[3] in the garden.

"Are you afraid I'm going to fall into your mini-pool or something?" I ask and try to smile, although actually my heart is beating fast[4]. Somehow I get the feeling[5] that Mia is going to tell me something bad – it's the way she's been behaving for the last quarter of an hour or so. First off, she shoves[6] a big packet of chocolate biscuits at me, watches while I chomp through[7] them one after the other, doesn't even contradict[8] me when I say that the newest film with her favourite actor is boring ... Something's not right here![9]

"Natalie, you've got to be strong now," she repeats and pulls me towards the bench under the cherry tree. I've still got a fake[10] smile stuck on my face as she sits down next to me and puts her arm around me. "Now, working on[11] a catastrophe scale of 1 to 100, what would be your number 100, like, the worst possible thing for you?"

I get annoyed. "Mia, I'm not up for[12] any more of these stupid psychology-tests. I think it's great that you want to become a psychologist, but why do I always have to be your guinea pig[13]?" She pulls me back onto the bench.

. . . .

1 **brave** – *mutig, stark*
2 **to whisper** – *flüstern*
3 **paddling pool** – *Planschbecken*
4 **my heart is beating fast** – *ich habe Herzklopfen*
5 **to get the feeling that ...** – *den Eindruck bekommen, dass ...*
6 **to shove sth. at sb.** (Umgangsprache) – *jdm. etw. in die Hand drücken*
7 **to chomp through** (Umgangsprache) – hier: *verdrücken*
8 **to contradict sb.** – *jdm. widersprechen*
9 **something's not right here** (Redewendung) – *irgendetwas stimmt hier nicht!*
10 **fake** – *unecht*
11 **working on** – hier: *auf*
12 **to be up for sth.** – *auf etw. Lust haben*
13 **guinea pig** – hier: *Versuchskaninchen*

"Hey, calm down[1]! I'm not talking about a test here, I'm talking about real life. So, come on: what would be your number 100?"
"OK," I think to myself[2] and reach for the last biscuit. I'll do it. I knit my brow[3], pretend that[4] I'm giving it a lot of thought[5], and then shout: "An A[6] in English! That would be a disaster – it would make me look like a real loser."
"Good one[7]!" sighs Mia, and keeps looking at me.
"Alright, something else then," I say – and decide never to eat an entire pack of chocolate biscuits ever again. Mia is looking at me, worried[8], and wants to know if I'm okay. I nod and think hard[9] about what I could offer her for her scale of catastrophes. Then I hit on[10] something that I saw in a film last week. I giggle. "Alright, the ultimate catastrophe for me would be to get a patchy tan[11] whilst sunbathing[12]. Think about it: brown legs at the front, white at the back. What does that look like![13]" I laugh out loud and then ask: "And what does my psychologist have to say about that?"
Mia shrugs her shoulders and then looks almost insulted[14] for a moment. "I just thought I'd find a nice way of telling you about it[15], but if that's the way you feel about it, we'll just go for it[16] right now."

· · · · · · · · ·
1   **to calm down** - *sich beruhigen*
2   **to think to oneself** - *sich denken*
3   **to knit one's brown** - *die Stirn runzeln*
4   **to pretend that** - *so tun als ob*
5   **to give sth. a lot of thought** - *lange über etw. nachdenken*
6   **A** – hier: (die Schulnote) *Eins*
7   **Good one!** (Umgangssprache) – *Selten so gelacht!*
8   **worried** – *besorgt*
9   **to think hard** – *schwer überlegen*
10 **to hit on sth.** - *auf etw. kommen*
11 **patchy tan** – *fleckige Sonnenbräune*
12 **sunbathing** – *Sonnenbaden*
13 **What does that look like!** (Redewendung) – *Wie sieht das denn aus!*
14 **insulted** – *beleidigt*
15 **a nice way of telling you about it** – *eine schonende Art, dir das beizubringen*
16 **to go for it** (Umgangssprache) – *reinhauen, an etw. (direkt) rangehen*

"Come on! Stop these stupid little games, you're ruining[1] my Saturday," I reply, "and seriously, I'm meeting Felix afterwards and I'm really not up for a bad mood."

"Oh, right, Felix," she says in a voice that gives me goose bumps[2] and holds up her mobile phone in front of my face.

"No!" I shout after having looked at the display for a while refusing to believe it[3].

"No, I don't buy that[4]. That can't be right."

"Yes it can," replies Mia, "I'm afraid it's true – pictures don't lie. And anyway, I recorded the video myself. I did try to prepare you for this nice and carefully[5], but you ..."

"200!" I say in a monotone[6] voice.

"200 what?" asks Mia.

"That's 200 on your catastrophe scale," I sigh[7]. The video is, unfortunately, impossible to misinterpret[8]. In fact, it would be impossible for the video to be more impossible to interpret; and the crystal clear picture, too, showing Felix, my lovely blond Felix with his unbelievably beautiful blue eyes – Felix, who yesterday was still swearing true love[9] to me and saying that he couldn't imagine life without me – Felix, now to be seen snogging[10] that overdressed[11] girl from the other class in our year[12], Vanessa, as if he was trying

. . . .
1 **to ruin** - *verderben*
2 **to give sb. goose bumps** – *bei jdm. eine Gänsehaut verursachen*
3 **refusing to believe** - *ungläubig*
4 **I don't buy that!** (Umgangssprache) – *Das kaufe ich dir nicht ab!*
5 **nice and carefully** – *schön vorsichtig*
6 **monotone** – *monoton, tonlos*
7 **to sigh** – *seufzen*
8 **impossible to misinterpret** – *absolut eindeutig*
9 **to swear true love** – *wahre Liebe schwören*
10 **to snog** – *knutschen*
11 **overdressed** – *aufgedonnert*
12 **the other class in our year** – *Parallelklasse*

to make it onto the silver screen[1]. It's enough to make you cry[2].

"I broke off after exactly 12 seconds – I didn't want them to work out that[3] I was filming them; not that that was very likely because they were both, like, pretty[4] busy."

"Haha, very funny," I mumble.[5]

"And then the stupid bus came after a quarter of an hour, so I have absolutely no idea how long they kept on at it[6]."

"Perhaps they're still stuck to each other[7]," I say. It's odd: it doesn't actually hurt that much to see my worst nightmares come true; I was always scared of losing Felix. Every girl I know is crazy about him[8], some more openly than others. Then again, I never really understood it anyway – what it was about me that made him fall in love with me. I'm not exactly the star of our class!

"You're not crying," remarks[9] Mia, confused[10], "are you sure you don't want to cry?"

"Yes, I'm very sure!" I shout, "Mia, there's nothing wrong with psychology, and I'm very sorry if I'm not behaving like in your psychology books: but right now, I don't want to cry. All I want to do is yell[11]!"

But since Mia's dad had a nightshift and has just gone to bed, I decide not to. Anyway, it's best to conserve my energy[12], especially

· · · · · · · · ·

1 **as if he was trying to make it onto the silver screen** – hier: *kinoreif*
2 **It's enough to make you cry** (Umgangssprache) – *Es ist zum Heulen*
3 **to work out that** (Umgangssprache) – *mitkriegen, dass*
4 **pretty busy** (Umgangssprache) – *ganz schön beschäftigt*
5 **to mumble** – *murmeln*
6 **to keep on at it** (Umgangssprache) – *so weitermachen*
7 **stuck to each other** – *aneinander geklebt*
8 **to be crazy about so.** – *für jdn. schwärmen*
9 **to remark** – *feststellen*
10 **confused** – *irritiert*
11 **to yell** – *brüllen*
12 **to conserve energy** – hier: *Energie aufbewahren*

my negative energy – for Felix! The dirty cheat[1]! That's just what he deserves[2].

"Should I go and talk to Felix?" asks Mia gently[3] as she walks with me to the tram stop twenty minutes later.

"I mean, I could go and tell him how stupid he's been. You know, what with him actually only loving you etc[4]." She tacks on[5] this last sentence after a noticeable[6] pause.

"That's nice of you, but I think this is something I've got to take care of myself[7]", I reply and hope that I sound relaxed about it. The only thing is that I've got no idea what to do. I only know one thing: I'm not going to let myself get treated like that[8]. So yesterday he's swearing true love and then snogging Vanessa for like fifteen minutes at the least! He's just asking for it[9].

I say goodbye to Mia with a kiss on the cheek[10], to the left and to the right, and then dash off[11]: I want to get the tram that's just stopping because I've just seen Leo in it. If I'm at all lucky[12] then at least this last little sprint will be successful and Leo will say something nice to me: after all, Mia told me that he was kind of in love with me earlier on in the year and right now I just need someone who likes me.

• • • • • • • • •

1 **cheat** – *Betrüger*
2 **That's just what he deserves** (Redewendung) – *Das hat er verdient!*
3 **gently** – hier: *vorsichtig*
4 **etc** – hier: *und so*
5 **to tack on** (Umgangssprache) – *hinzufügen*
6 **noticeable** – *spürbar*
7 **to take care of sth. oneself** – *etw. selbst erledigen*
8 **I'm not going to let myself get treated like that** (Redewendung) – *Mit mir nicht!*
9 **He's just asking for it!** (Redewendung) – *Das schreit nach Rache!*
10 **kiss on the cheek** – *Kuss auf die Wange*
11 **to dash off** – *losrennen*
12 **If I'm at all lucky** – *Mit ein wenig Glück*

TR. 02 "Phew!" I say as I fall onto the seat next to Leo a few seconds later, "that was a close one[1]."

"That was one hell of a show![2]" he says approvingly[3]. "In fact, did you know that we're currently on the look-out for[4] people with your kind of talent for our mixed football eleven? We need people who can sprint, and then we can teach you how to score[5] – that's a promise! It'd be great if you'd play with us."

"Thanks Leo" I say, smiling at him, "that's really nice of you. But I'm not sure that football is, like, my thing. I do know someone who really wants to play for you guys, though!"

I'm very satisfied with myself[6] as I lean back[7]. The tram I'm in isn't travelling in my direction – in fact, it's travelling in completely the opposite direction[8] – but apart from that, everything is going very well. The thing is, I've just had a great idea, so I add something: "All the more since you're there." Leo looks at me confused, but I just smile.

"Come on, no need to make such a secret out of it," he says after a pause, "who do you mean?"

I need to speed up[9] because I don't know exactly at which stop he gets out – he could be off[10] any minute. So I go for it and whisper to him: "It's Vanessa! But don't tell anyone I told you. She's crazy about you – she said she'd never been so in love before."

. . . .

1 **That was a close one** (Redewendung) – *Das war knapp!*
2 **One hell of a show!** (Redewendung) – hier: *Superleistung!*
3 **approvingly** - *anerkennend*
4 **on the look-out for** – *auf der Suche nach*
5 **to score** – hier: *Tore schießen*
6 **satisfied with oneself** – *zufrieden (mit sich selbst)*
7 **to lean back** – *sich zurücklehnen*
8 **opposite direction** - *Gegenrichtung*
9 **to speed up** – *sich beeilen, Gas geben*
10 **to be off** (Umgangssprache) – *weg sein*

"Vanessa?" he asks disbelievingly[1].

That's not the sound of overwhelming enthusiasm[2]. Then again, maybe that's because he hasn't had much experience with girls just yet – that's certainly the impression I get[3]. He's been in our class for half a year and, as far as we know, doesn't have a girlfriend. So it could well be[4] that I've scared him. You can never be quite sure what boys are thinking.

"Vanessa from the other class?" he asks, "The one with long, dark hair?"

"Yep, her," I smile and just about manage to stop myself saying[5] something unfortunate[6] like "Yeah, that stupid cow who got caught sticking her tongue down Felix' throat[7] for a full quarter of an hour." Leo looks at me inquisitively[8]; I feel slightly awkward[9] and squirm in my seat[10]. Perhaps it wasn't the best idea I've ever had ... but I should have thought about that beforehand[11].

"You mean, like, the cool one. I mean, how should I ..." He swallows. I put my hand on his arm to calm him down.

"You know what? Vanessa is actually[12] quite nervous – you wouldn't think so, but she is. Believe me, she is!" I leave my hand on his arm for a little bit; you know, so that he gets, like, practice[13] and learns how it feels with a girl; and while I'm doing that, I smile at

• • • • • • • •

1 **disbelievingly** – *ungläubig*
2 **overwhelming enthusiasm** – *überwältigende Begeisterung*
3 **that's certainly the impression I get** (Redewendung) – *so scheint es jedenfalls*
4 **It could well be that ...** (Redewendung) – *Es kann durchaus sein, dass ...*
5 **to stop oneself saying sth.** – *sich etw. verkneifen*
6 **unfortunate** – *unvorteilhaft*
7 **to stick one's tongue down someone's throat** (Umgangssprache) – *jem. die Zunge in den Hals stecken*
8 **inquisitively** – *fragend*
9 **awkward** – *unbehaglich*
10 **to squirm on one's seat** – *auf seinem Sitz herumrutschen*
11 **beforehand** – *vorher*
12 **actually** – *in Wirklichkeit*
13 **to get practice** – *Übung bekommen*

him encouragingly[1]. This, however, has the result of making him turn red. Jesus Christ! He won't get very far with Vanessa like this, you can be sure of that. After a while, his skin goes back to normal and he pulls himself together[2].

"I don't know whether I'm the right guy for Vanessa, you know. I mean, what should I say to her? I can't just, like, go up and talk to her, can I? What do you think?"

"Of course you can!" is what I would like to say, but instead I remain silent. That's the thing with Leo – I think he really might be too shy. It's a shame I didn't run across[3] Olli: he would be pretty enthusiastic about Vanessa and would be guaranteed to get on the phone to her and get her to go on a date with him. And then Felix would be left with nobody[4]! Perhaps I should tell Leo now that it's all a big mistake and that he'd be better off forgetting everything[5]… But I just can't do that. He's smiling so nicely the whole time and I don't want to disappoint him. I know how horrible disappointment feels – I've been feeling it for the past half-hour. Oh no – Leo's standing up to get off!

"I'm getting off here," he explains.

"Wait a sec[6]!" I shout after him, "Where do you have your training sessions? And when?"

· · · · · · · · ·
1 **encouragingly** – *aufmunternd*
2 **to pull oneself together** – *sich fassen*
3 **to run across sb.** – *jdm. über den Weg laufen*
4 **to be left with nobody** – *das Nachsehen haben*
5 **he'd be better off forgetting everything** – *er sollte besser alles vergessen*
6 **sec** – *Sekunde* (Abkürzung für ‚*second*')

TR. 03 "Football training?" My mum shakes her head: "Natalie, we had agreed that[1] you were going to mow the lawn[2] today. And besides that, you've been promising me for[3] the last three weeks that you were going to tidy up your room[4]. And besides *that*,

Love-Question 1
☑ INBOX
from Mia Mobile

Hey babe! Hope u r
not 2 sad about
Felix. Saw that Leo
was on the tram —
what did he say? x

we've been wanting[5] to try out one of those lovely board games you got last Christmas. And since when have you been interested in football anyway?"

From what she says, it would appear that my mum is[6] not really very happy with my idea of spending Saturday afternoon at football training. So I pick up where she leaves off: "Yes, well, that's the point. I don't really like football," I admit[7], "but it's not like I want to go. It's kind of a school-thing I've got to go to. You see, someone dropped out[8], so I *have* to go."

As far as I can see, that's not a real lie[9] and, because I stressed[10] the word "have" and the whole thing suddenly sounds pretty official, my mum just sighs and says: "OK, but on Sunday you're going to stay here and tidy up your room, football or not[11]!"

Training doesn't begin until five o' clock, so that gives me enough

· · · · · · · ·

1 **we had agreed that ...** – *wir hatten ausgemacht, dass ...*
2 **to mow the lawn** – *den Rasen mähen*
3 **you've been promising me for the last three weeks that ...** – *du hast mir seit drei Wochen versprochen, dass ...*
4 **to tidy up one's room** - *sein Zimmer aufräumen*
5 **we've been wanting to ...** – *wir wollten ...*
6 **it would appear that my mum is ...** – *augenscheinlich ist meine Mutter ...*
7 **to admit** – *zugeben*
8 **to drop out** – *ausfallen*
9 **that's not a real lie** – *das ist nicht mal richtig geschwindelt*
10 **to stress** – hier: *betonen*
11 **football or not!** – *Fußball hin oder her!*

time for a quick detour[1] to Martinstraße, which is where Felix'
parents have a small stationers[2]. While I'm on the way, I think
about whether it really is a good idea to just show up[3], knowing
what I do from Mia. Now, I know she would advise me against it[4],
but there's no choice: I have to do it, I have to see him.

"We're just closing[5]!" shouts Felix as I go into the shop. Then he
recognises me and smiles embarrassedly[6].

"Sorry, I thought it was another customer who absolutely had to
buy a green-yellow-blue rubber with comic figures before closing
time," he says.

"A green-yellow-blue rubber with comic figures!" I laugh. Here
we are, standing opposite one another. Felix is smiling his confident[7] smile, the smile I fell in love with all those months ago. He's
crossed his arms over his chest[8], he's still wearing the friendship-
bracelet[9] I gave him for his birthday on his right-hand wrist ... Uh,
this is all so messed up[10]. If I could just get that stupid video out of
my head! Those twelve awful seconds ...

"So ... er, what's up" he asks.

Now, what I should really do is to look at him coldly, ask for two
exercise books – one squared and one lined with a margin[11] – and
slam[12] down the cash on the counter before disappearing out of his

· · · · · · · · ·

1 **detour** – *Abstecher*
2 **stationers** – *Schreibwarengeschäft*
3 **to just show up** – *einfach vorbeischauen*
4 **to advise sb. against sth.** – *jdm. von etw. abraten*
5 **We're just closing!** – *Wir schließen gerade!*
6 **embarrassedly** – *verlegen*
7 **confident** – *selbstbewusst*
8 **to cross one's arms over one's chest** – *die Arme vor der Brust verschränken*
9 **friendship-bracelet** – *Freundschaftsbändchen*
10 **messed up** (Umgangssprache) – *bescheuert*
11 **with a margin** – *mit Rand*
12 **to slam** – *knallen*

life forever, throwing a curt[1] "See ya!" behind me as I swan out[2]. Instead, I hear myself saying: "What time are we going to meet tonight? We were going to get together ..."

"Tonight?" he asks.

"Yes. We can't really meet yesterday evening can we?" I reply. I'm pretty sure that he'll have to show his true colours[3] now. Or at least try some silly excuse[4], that I won't let count[5], of course. And then I'll tell exactly what I think of him snogging that Vanessa. And then ...

"Of course, tonight," he laughs, "Natalie, we had agreed on it."

I notice myself getting weak. It's obvious: Felix loves me and only me. What he did with Vanessa can only have been a moment of complete madness[6]; perhaps it was the heat of the midday sun that made him momentarily utterly[7] incapable of[8] thinking clearly ... I'll have to talk to Mia. As an aspiring[9] psychologist, she's bound to[10] know something about it. Felix takes me in his arms. It's like heaven for a moment, just like it used to be. Then a mobile phone rings. It takes me a while to work out[11] that it's Felix' mobile that is ringing and that it's got a completely new ring-tone. And it's a corny[12] one too: "Love forever"! "Aren't you going to answer[13]?"

"It wasn't important," he says as it stops, "the only important thing is us. Hey, would it be alright if we met a bit later this evening?

· · · · · · · · ·

1 **curt** – *knapp, schroff*
2 **to swan out** – *majestätisch herausschweben*
3 **to show one's true colours** – *Farbe bekennen*
4 **excuse** – *Ausrede*
5 **to let sth. count** – *etw. gelten lassen*
6 **complete madness** – *völliger geistiger Verwirrung*
7 **utterly** – *ganz, völlig*
8 **incapable of doing sth.** – *außerstande, etw. zu tun*
9 **aspiring** – *aufstrebend*
10 **she's bound to ...** – *Sie wird bestimmt ...*
11 **to work out** (Umgangssprache) – *kapieren*
12 **corny** – *kitschig*
13 **to answer** – hier: *rangehen*

I've got to clean the shop and ..." The mobile rings again.
Felix can't stop himself. "It must be my mother," he says, "and apart from that[1], I've got to do the shopping and she's probably remembered something very important that I absolutely have to buy."
He answers the phone with a brusque[2] "Yeah?" I pretend to be looking at the posters on the door, but of course I'm actually cocking my ears[3]. My heart starts beating fast again; after all, I can't really imagine that Felix has given that ring-tone to his mother's phone number. He smiles at me, holds his hand over the phone and whispers: "I told you – my mum!" Then he talks into the telephone: "It's not convenient[4] at the moment. Can I call you back later?"
I smile a big smile at him as he hangs up. It's difficult, but I somehow manage to pull up the corners of my mouth and look nice, despite that face that, inside, I'm a ticking time bomb of rage[5]. After all, it's pretty clear that Felix has not just been on the phone to[6] his mother: I've just noticed her standing in front of the shop talking to on old married couple with a black poodle. I wonder how long it will take Felix to figure that one out[7].
"I'm supposed to buy a pound of Swiss chard[8]," he sighs, "whatever that is. You know, my mum's got a real knack for ringing[9] whenever it's not convenient." Now he's got his arm around me and asks: "Weren't we just about to kiss?"

. . . .

1 **apart from that** – *außerdem*
2 **brusque** – *knapp, schroff*
3 **to cock one's ears** – *die Ohren spitzen*
4 **it's not convenient** – *es passt gerade nicht*
5 **I am a ticking time bomb of rage** – *ich könnte jeden Moment vor Wut platzen*
6 **to be on the phone to sb.** – *mit jdm. am Telefon sprechen*
7 **to figure sth. out** (Umgangssprache) – *etw. kapieren*
8 **Swiss chard** – *Mangold*
9 **to have a knack for doing sth.** – *ein Talent dafür haben, etw. zu tun*

"No, I don't think so," I say, writhing[1] out of his arms, "and you can find out what Swiss chard is in just a second, by the way, because your mum's been chatting away[2] in front of the shop for the last five minutes."

TR. 04 I'm running late as I get to the sports fields; but it was well worth it[3] to see the look of surprise[4] on Felix' face and hear his absolutely pathetic[5] attempt[6] at an excuse, and then his mother, who said "Vanessa told me to say a special hello" as she came in … And the best bit[7]: the way he ran after me for three full hours, shouting about how he only loved me and how there was nothing going on with Vanessa[8] and how he hardly[9] knew her and blah blah blah. What I'd really like to do is to ring Mia and tell her everything hot off the press[10], but I'll have to do that later. The most important thing to do at the moment is to get Leo to start something with Vanessa. Then Felix will see just how badly it hurts[11]! A couple of lads[12] are kicking a ball around, but apart from that there's nobody. Great! It seems that nothing is going to go right today. Did Leo tell me some rubbish about football training for the pleasure of laughing himself silly[13] because I've turned up here like a good little girl[14]? It's not really his way, but you can

· · · · · · · · ·

1 **to writhe** – *sich winden*
2 **to be chatting away** – *quatschen*
3 **it was well worth it** – *es war es wert*
4 **look of surprise** – *Ausdruck der Überraschung*
5 **pathetic** – *erbärmlich, lächerlich*
6 **attempt** – *Versuch*
7 **the best bit** – *das Allerbeste*
8 **there was nothing going on with Vanessa** – *mit Vanessa sei nichts*
9 **hardly** – *kaum*
10 **hot off the press** – *brühwarm*
11 **how badly it hurts** – *wie weh das tut*
12 **lad** (Umgangssprache) – *Junge, Typ*
13 **to laugh oneself silly** (Redewendung) – *sich krank lachen*
14 **like a good little boy/girl** – (ironisch) *schön brav*

never be quite sure with lads. Before, however, I sink into a deep depression; I force myself to be positive: after all, Leo could have run into Vanessa[1] and taken the opportunity to confess his love to[2] her. Then she works out that, in reality, she only has eyes for Leo[3] and doesn't love Felix. Before you know it[4], she's dumped him and he's on his knees begging me to take him back.

"Natalie!" I hear someone shout and, just like that[5], my beautiful dream vanishes[6]. I turn round and there's Leo. No Vanessa, but he's completely out of breath[7].

"Training is cancelled! But I couldn't ring you because I didn't have your mobile number. So I stopped off at your place[8] but no-one was there, and then ..."

```
Love-Question 2
☑ INBOX
from Mia Mobile

Hi Nat! Have u seen
Felix? Where r u now?
What r u doing? Text
back! ;-)
```

"Oh," I say, almost touched[9], "you came especially[10] to my house? That's very nice of you." He's sweet, but it's embarrassing. He's going red again; I'll have to get him to stop doing that on the double[11] – I don't think Vanessa will find it as sweet as I do.

"I hope you're not angry because I forgot to tell you," he says. I shake my head. In fact, I'm quite pleased at not having to play

· · · · · · · · ·

1 **to run into sb.** – jdn. zufällig treffen
2 **to confess one's love to sb.** – jdm. seine Liebe gestehen
3 **to only have eyes for sb.** – nur Augen für jdn. haben
4 **before you know it** (Umgangssprache) – noch bevor man sich versieht
5 **just like that** (Umgangssprache) – ruck, zuck
6 **to vanish** – verschwinden
7 **out of breath** – außer Atem
8 **at your place** (Umgangssprache) – bei dir zu Hause
9 **almost touched** – fast gerührt
10 **especially** - extra
11 **on the double** (Umgangssprache) – schleunigst, umgehend

football, although I don't need to let him know that.

"It's fine!" I say and think about how to change subjects onto Vanessa as quickly as possible. The best thing would be for him to meet her this evening, of course; after all, after what happened between me and Felix just now, he'll most likely go running straight into her open arms[1] – and we have put a stop to that with every means at our disposal[2].

"I think you should be a striker!" says Leo, suddenly.

"Sorry?" I don't understand. He laughs.

"Well, you've got the right facial expression for it. You're kind of a ..." – he pauses for a second – "you look like a winner. A real winner!"

I nod. "You bet![3] That's how I feel too," I claim[4]. Winner? Yeah, right![5] There's no trace of victory[6] at the moment. Unless, of course, I manage to get Leo and Vanessa together: but it would be too unromantic to talk to Leo about his feelings for Vanessa on a dusty football pitch, so I suggest that we go and have an ice-cream. I know, it's not very original, but I can't think of anything better right now, so it will have to do. Leo, however, doesn't bat an eyelid[7]: he came by bike and, since the nearest ice-cream parlour is a good way[8] from here, I swing myself onto the rack[9] and let my mind wander[10] as Leo pedals[11] hard.

· · · · · · · · ·

1 **to go running into sb.'s arms** – *bei jdm. Trost suchen*
2 **and we have to put a stop to that with every means at our disposal** – *und das gilt es mit allen Mitteln zu verhindern*
3 **You bet!** (Umgangssprache) – *Exakt!, Aber klar!*
4 **to claim** - *behaupten*
5 **Yeah, right!** – *Von wegen!*
6 **no trace of victory** – *von Sieg keine Spur*
7 **to not bat an eyelid** – *nicht mit der Wimper zucken*
8 **a good way** – *ein gutes Stück*
9 **rack** – hier: *Gepäckträger*
10 **to let one's mind wander** – *seinen Gedanken freien Lauf lassen*
11 **to pedal** – *in die Pedale treten*

TR. 05 It'd be great if Felix could see us now; he'd be bursting with jealousy. Then I remember that he's in love with Vanessa at the moment, so it'd probably suit him very well[1] to see us together now. Damn! "Stop!" I shout as I realise that Leo is about to turn into Martinstraße. He turns round.

> Love-Question 3
> ☑ INBOX
> from Mia Mobile
>
> Hi Nat! Sorry 2 hear
> about thing with Fe-
> lix. How is football
> practice? ;-)

"But that's the shortest way, and we wanted to ..."

"No," I say, "I don't want an ice-cream anymore. Let's go and play mini-golf instead. Turn around!" Now, mini-golf is not exactly at the top of my list of favourite free-time activities, but it remains the lesser of two evils[2]; the mini-golf course is quite some distance away from Martinstraße. And if Leo thinks I'm being catty[3] that's fine – I can't be concerned with that[4] right now. There are only three things that are important at the moment: Felix can't see me with Leo; Leo has to fall in love with Vanessa; and Vanessa has to fall in love with Leo! Of course, mini-golf on Saturdays means that hordes[5] of families have occupied[6] the course with gaggles[7] of whinging[8] kids who can't yet grip the club[9] properly and keep shouting for lemonade.

. . . .

1 **to suit sb. well** – *jdm. gelegen kommen*
2 **the lesser of two evils** – *das kleinere Übel*
3 **catty** – *zickig*
4 **to be concerned with sth.** – *Rücksicht auf etw. nehmen*
5 **horde** – *Horde*
6 **to occupy** – *besetzen*
7 **gaggle** – *Schar*
8 **whinging** – *quengelnd*
9 **club** – hier: *Schläger*

"I'm sorry," says the young lady at the kiosk, "but we don't have a single club left at the moment. You can try again in half an hour or so – you'll probably have better luck then."

I think about whether it would be a good idea to suggest ice-cream again, but I reckon Leo will probably think I've gone completely crazy[1], so I keep quiet. We sit down on a bench in front of the golf course and, for a while, neither of us says anything. Ha! The world could be such a beautiful place, I think to myself. If Felix were here sitting next to me and if this stupid Vanessa girl were to fall head-over-heels in love[2] with Leo immediately ... But just sitting around won't make it happen[3]. "Vanessa loves you!" I blurt out[4]. It almost seems as if Leo is grinning; at least he's not going red this time! It's probably some kind of[5] familiarisation[6], as Mia would put it. "It's true, you can believe me," I add. Now, everyone knows that you've got to strike while the iron is hot[7], and now would seem to be the right moment to talk about love. It's even quite romantic, sitting here under a huge chestnut tree[8] and listening to the cheese song[9] on the radio in the kiosk ... I'm pretty sure that there'll be a gorgeous[10] sunset in a couple of hours: you know, glowing red[11], the whole kit and caboodle[12]; enough to make even Leo get romantic. So it's annoying that my mobile rings at this of

· · · · · · · · ·

1 **Leo will probably think I've gone completely crazy** – *Leo wird mich dann wohl für völlig durchgeknallt halten*
2 **to fall head-over-heels in love** – *sich heftigst verlieben*
3 **but just sitting around won't make it happen!** – *allein vom Rumsitzen wird das bestimmt nichts!*
4 **to blurt out** – *herausplatzen*
5 **some kind of ...** – *so eine Art ...*
6 **familiarisation** – *Gewöhnung*
7 **to strike while the iron is hot** – *das Eisen schmieden, solange es heiß ist*
8 **chestnut tree** – *Kastanienbaum*
9 **cheesy song** – *kitschiges Lied*
10 **gorgeous** – *traumhaft*
11 **glowing red** – *glutrot*
12 **the whole kit and caboodle** (Umgangssprache) – *alles Drum und Dran*

all times[1]. I try and ignore it but, as it could be Felix ready to ask me for forgiveness[2] and swear true love to me, I take a look to see who's calling. The number is withheld[3], so I answer just in case[4] because when Felix calls from the shop the number doesn't show up. But it's not Felix, it's Mia, completely hectic and very excited. "Listen to this: a mixed table football tournament!" She shouts so loud that I hold the phone away from my ear: I'm not up for risking my hearing just because Mia feels like shouting. "And here's the great bit: the winning couple gets a candle-light dinner!"

"Yeah, great ..." I mumble. God knows why she is a) so excited and b) going on about[5] table football and c) ...

"Are you still there?" she asks. Thankfully she's back down to normal volume[6].

"Yes, I still am. Er, Mia, this is all very exciting and stuff[7] but ... can we talk about it another time? I'm kind of ..." I think about whether to tell her about Leo or not, but Mia just keeps talking.

"Felix and Vanessa are in it too! Natalie, you've got to come over and take a look. You have to see it to believe it[8]! By the way, I'm the one who has to draw[9] the couples for the tournament.

"Where?" is all I can ask.

"In the park next to the youth centre. It starts at seven and Felix and Vanessa will be playing in half an hour or so. She's got herself completely done up[10] again – just her style. The psychologist in me

· · · · · · · · ·

1 **at this of all times** – *ausgerechnet jetzt*
2 **forgiveness** – *Verzeihung*
3 **withheld** – *unterdrückt*
4 **just in case** – *vorsichtshalber*
5 **to go on about sth.** – *von etw. schwafeln*
6 **volume** – *Lautstärke*
7 **and stuff** (Umgangssprache) – *und so*
8 **you have to see it to believe it** (Redewendung) – *das musst du mit eigenen Augen gesehen haben*
9 **to draw** – hier: *auslosen*
10 **done up** (Umgangssprache) – *aufgebrezelt*

would say ..."

"Yes, I get you. Thanks for ringing – I'll think of something¹," I mumble and hang up. Damn! I'm sitting here next to Leo while Felix and Vanessa are about to win a candlelight dinner. Something has to happen – and it has to happen soon! I just wish I knew what!

The woman at the kiosk waves over to us²:"I've just got a load of clubs back – you can take your pick³."

Leo looks at me inquisitively. He looks really nice as he brushes his dark hair back with his hand. "Shall we?" he asks.

"Hmm," I say and notice how embarrassed I am, "I know this is really stupid, but somehow I'm not so into⁴ mini-golf right now." If he thinks I'm a stupid cow, I'll understand it immediately. I'm starting to think that I am one. I try to smile and take his hand. "Leo, I'd much rather play table football with you. In the park next to the youth centre there's a tournament this evening; my friend Mia just told me about it. Would you go with me? Please Leo? Vanessa's there ..." Perhaps that'll decide it⁵. Whatever the case, Leo says he wanted to stop by⁶ the youth centre this evening anyway and that we can watch the tournament.

• • • • • • • • •

1 **I'll think of sth.** – *Ich lasse mir etw. einfallen*
2 **to wave over to sb.** – *jdm. zuwinken*
3 **to take one's pick** – *sich etw. aussuchen*
4 **to be into sth.** (Umgangssprache) – *auf etw. Lust haben*
5 **to decide sth.** – hier: *den Ausschlag geben*
6 **to stop by** – *vorbeischauen*

"Leo, you're a great guy," I say as I sit back down on the rack and Leo pedals off. The atmosphere between us at the moment is great and for that reason I decide to strike the iron again: "Vanessa thinks you're great, too. You know,

```
Love-Question 4
☑ INBOX
from Mia Mobile


Hey babe! R u co-
ming 2 the tournament
then? x
```

she's been in love with you for a while now, but she doesn't know how to tell you. But I've told you all that anyway." Leo doesn't react to this at all. I wonder whether he understood everything I just shouted into his ear, so I repeat – with a little more volume – what I just said: "Leo, honestly, she's in love with you." He comes up to a red traffic light[1] and turns round and looks at me.

"And what should I do, in your opinion?" he asks. Our eyes cross[2]. "I didn't know you had green eyes!" I say, astonished[3]. That just slipped out[4] and has, of course, nothing to do with his question. So I quickly add something: "All you've got to do is talk to her. She might react strangely at first, but you know that she won't mean it badly."

TR. 06 A couple of minutes later, we arrive at the park next to the youth centre – and by this stage[5], I myself almost believe that Vanessa is madly in love[6] with Leo too.

· · · · · · · · ·

1 **traffic light** – *Ampel*
2 **our eyes cross** – *unsere Blicke treffen sich*
3 **astonished** – *erstaunt*
4 **to slip out** – *rausrutschen*
5 **by this stage** – *zu diesem Zeitpunkt*
6 **madly in love** – *total verknallt*

"Hey, you're finally here," whispers Mia as she gives me a hug, "but why did you bring Leo with you? I thought you'd want to speak to Fe ..."

"Yes, I do," I whisper back, "but Leo here is madly in love with Vanessa and I think we should help him out; and perhaps Felix will notice ..."

Someone is tapping[1] my shoulder. I jump[2] – is it Felix? No, it's Leo, and he wants to know if he should bring me something to drink.

"Yes, great idea," I say – that gives me a couple of minutes to talk to Mia alone. But Mia doesn't have time.

"Sorry Natalie, I'm a bit stressed out[3]," she says: "I've got to draw the couples for the tournament. It should have been Marilou's job, but since she's got such bad hayfever[4] she can't do it and they rang me, what with me living just a couple of streets down the road[5] ..."

"Hang on a sec![6] I say, interrupting[7] her, "I think I've just had the perfect idea!" "By the way," I say grinning as Leo returns with two bottles of lemonade, "I've just signed us up[8] for the tournament. You don't mind, do you?[9]" For a second, I think his chin is about to hit the floor[10], but then he gets a grip of himself again and smiles at me.

· · · · · · · · ·

1 **to tap** – *tippen*
2 **to jump** – hier: *zusammenfahren*
3 **to be stressed out** – *im Stress sein*
4 **hayfever** – *Heuschnupfen*
5 **what with me living just a couple of streets down the road** – *da ich ja nur paar Straßen weiter wohne*
6 **Hang on a sec!** (Redewendung) – *Stopp mal! Halt!*
7 **to interrupt** – *unterbrechen*
8 **to sign sb. up** – *jdn. anmelden*
9 **You don't mind, do you?** – *Du hast nichts dagegen, oder?*
10 **I think his chin is about to hit the floor** – *ich habe den Eindruck, dass ihm gleich die Kinnlade runterfällt*

"OK, but tell me what the chances[1] of you backing out[2] are."

"Hm, quite high, if I think of a better idea ..." I say, smiling and put my arm through his[3], "and anyway, everyone's always telling everyone to wait and see, to play it by ear[4]. And there's a prize, too!"

"OK, Natalie, then let's play it by ear," he says and passes me the bottle of lemonade, "and now you can tell me what there is to win."

"I'm not going to give that away[5]!" I say with an air of mystery[6]: "You'll soon find out. Now, let's see who's playing against who."

What is about to happen is, in all honesty, not fair-play[7]. In fact, you might even call it cheating[8], but it's all for a good cause[9] - without anyone noticing, Mia has marked Vanessa and Leo's two pieces of paper and then drawn them first.

Thanks Mia! I'll always remember that, thank you! I'm not bothered about the rest of the couples now; the only important thing is that Leo plays his part to perfection[10]. I elbow him gently[11]: "Don't you think that this must be fate[12]?"

"What, that you're playing with Felix?"

Whoops! I hadn't noticed that! I look at Leo uneasily[13]. Does he know more than I think?

. . . .

1 **the chances** – *die Wahrscheinlichkeit*
2 **to back out** – *abspringen*
3 **to put one's arm through sb.'s** – *sich bei jdm. ein-/unterhaken*
4 **to play it by ear** (Redewendung) – *flexibel bleiben, improvisieren*
5 **to give away** – hier: *verraten*
6 **with an air of mystery** – *geheimnisvoll*
7 **not fair-play** – *nicht fair*
8 **cheating** – *Schummeln, Mogeln*
9 **it's all for a good cause** (Redewendung) – *es dient schließlich einem guten Zweck*
10 **to play one's part to perfection** – *seine Rolle perfekt spielen*
11 **to elbow someone gently** – *jdn. leicht anstoßen*
12 **fate** – *Schicksal*
13 **uneasily** – *unsicher*

"Me and Felix?" I say this in an emphatically[1] casual[2] way: "How interesting ..."

"Yes, if I understood the results of the draw correctly."

This is absolute madness, I think to myself. Just how did Mia manage to get me and Felix playing together? Maybe we'll win that candle-light dinner and then he'll remember just how great things were between us. I could borrow Mia's really stylish[3] red dress for the occasion ...

Leo elbows me and this brings me back down to earth[4]: "Are you alright?" he asks.

"Yes, I'm fine thanks. I was just thinking about you and Vanessa playing together. It really does seem like fate is playing a part. It's as if it's meant to be[5]."

"I don't know ..." he mumbles, "could be, if that's the way you want to see it."

He seems relatively relaxed; I just hope that's the way it stays when he's standing opposite Vanessa and she looks him up and down[6] with her arrogant smile and tosses back her black hair – God, I hate her! That being the case, it would probably be a good idea to test out his self-confidence. If I'm dissatisfied with his reaction, I'll have to go and have a quick talk to Mia again – she will know how to turn Leo into a cool guy in no time at all[7].

"Leo!" I shout and look him straight in the eyes. He's got to last[8] for

· · · · · · · · ·

1 **emphatically** – *betont*
2 **casual** – *beiläufig*
3 **stylish** – *chic, modisch*
4 **to bring sb. back down to earth** – *jdn. auf den Boden der Tatsachen zurückholen*
5 **it's as if it's meant to be** (Redewendung) – *Es ist wie vorherbestimmt*
6 **to look sb. up and down** – *jdn. von oben bis unten mustern*
7 **in no time at all** – *ruck, zuck*
8 **to last** – hier: *aushalten, durchhalten*

at least ten seconds, I say to myself. Anything less just won't do [1]...
And, as it happens [2], he holds out fine. He even smiles back to me,
keeps eye-contact [3] for longer than ten seconds – in fact, it seems
like ages – and then something happens that really doesn't help me
at all: for a change, it's me who goes bright red [4]. It's horrifically [5]
embarrassing and to avoid false interpretations, I turn round. This
also gives me the chance [6] to look for Felix. He's nowhere to be
seen, though! There's just Vanessa standing next to Mia talking to
her non-stop; she's probably on at her to [7] re-do the draw so that
she can play with Felix. While all that's going on, my skin has
returned to a half-way [8] normal colour and I turn to Leo.

"Are you really sure that Vanessa is into me [9]? It seems to me that
she hasn't even noticed I'm here [10].

"Of course Leo!" I say to calm him down: "You know what? Girls
don't show it as much as boys – that's why you've got to make the
first move [11]. Then it'll be fine – promise!" That sounds all well and
good [12], but I suddenly get worried when he goes off to warm up [13]
with Vanessa.

"And?" asks Mia as she sits down next to me a few moments later:
"I reckon that your Felix won't have much of a chance with Vanessa
now – she's crazy about Leo!"

. . . .

1 **just won't do** (Redewendung) – *geht gar nicht*
2 **as it happens** – *in der Tat, tatsächlich*
3 **to keep eye-contact** – *Augenkontakt halten*
4 **bright red** – *knallrot*
5 **horrifically** – *grauenhaft*
6 **this also gives me the chance to ...** – *bei der Gelegenheit kann ich auch ...*
7 **to be on at sb. to do sth.** – *jdm. damit in den Ohren liegen, etw. zu tun*
8 **half-way** – *halbwegs, einigermaßen*
9 **to bei into sb.** (Umgangssprache) – *auf jdn .stehen*
10 **she hasn't even noticed I'm here** - *sie hat mich nicht mal wahrgenommen*
11 **to make the first move** – *den ersten Schritt machen*
12 **that sounds all well and good, but ...** (Redewendung) – *Das klingt zwar alles schön und gut, aber ...*
13 **to warm up** – *hier: sich einspielen*

"I don't really know," I reply feebly[1], but Mia is probably right: Leo has really hit form[2] now. I can hear him laughing as he shouts something to Vanessa, and then I see her pretend to be angry and then give him a hug.

"Stupid cow!" I say under my breath[3] and Mia laughs.

"Hey, you're not jealous, are you?" she asks and elbows me in the ribs: "You know, when you got here with Leo, I did think there might be something going on with you two. And then the way you looked at each other just now[4]..."

"Rubbish!" I say indignantly[5]: "You're just imagining it[6]. The thing is: I had to train Leo up; you know, like, make him fit for Vanessa."

"Then that's all fine, no need to get angry," says Mia, satisfied[7], "after all, you wanted Vanessa to fall in love with Leo, and that seems to be going just fine. In fact, I'd say it will only take another half-hour or so."

Then she adds something. "Sorry about saying what I did – but I didn't just say it on gut feeling[8]: you are showing all the classic signs of being in love."

TR. 07 I jump up to leave. Sometimes Mia's psychologising[9] can really, really get on your nerves, especially when she's so wrong with it. Just to get things clear once and for all[10],

- - - - - - - -
1 **feebly** – *lahm, schwach*
2 **to hit form** – *zur Höchstform anlaufen*
3 **under one's breath** – *halblaut*
4 **just now** – *vorhin*
5 **indignantly** – *unwillig, entrüstet*
6 **you're just imagining it** – *das bildest du dir nur ein*
7 **satisfied** – *zufrieden*
8 **gut feeling** – *Bauchgefühl*
9 **psychologising** - *psychologisieren*
10 **once and for all** – *ein für alle Mal*

I say: "I really couldn't care less about Leo[1]. I just want Felix to come so that he sees what's going on."

Mia laughs at this. "Fine. He should be here in half an hour at the very latest. Then you two are playing. I'm crossing my fingers[2] for you to win. You're playing against Gülay and Adam, so you've got a good chance. Well, better than Vanessa and Leo in any case."

They're not doing very well at all. Their opponents keep on scoring goals[3], which seems not to bother Leo, but makes Vanessa shout: "Dammit[4]!" Suddenly, she breaks down in tears[5] in front of everybody. That's totally embarrassing, but what follows is even worse: Leo gives her a hug and talks to her gently. As far as I can see, he's going way overboard[6]. Well, OK, I did, like, tell him that Vanessa was in love with him. Then again, that's no reason to play the saviour[7]; and to hold onto her for, like, two and a half minutes – especially since Felix isn't even there yet. I've got to find him! I make my way through the crowd[8], see a few people from my class and the drama group I was in last year – but there's no sign of Felix. I gather up all my courage[9] and call him. First, it rings for ages[10]. Then, just as I'm about to hang up, he picks up and, instead of saying hi, answers with: "Are you back to normal yet?"

"What do you mean 'normal'?" I ask in return. I realise how I angry I am: "Anyway, you're the one who is causing all the trouble[11]

· · · · · · · · ·

1 **I really couldn't care less about Leo** – *Leo ist mir so was von egal*
2 **to cross one's fingers** – *die Daumen drücken*
3 **to score a goal** – *ein Tor schießen*
4 **Dammit!** (Umgangssprache) – *Verflixt!*
5 **to break down in tears** – *in Tränen ausbrechen*
6 **to go way overboard** (Umgangssprechen) – *total übertreiben*
7 **to play the saviour** – *den Retter vorspielen, einen auf Tröster machen*
8 **to make one's way through the crowd** – *sich einen Weg durch die Menge bahnen*
9 **to gather up all one's courage** – *seinen ganzen Mut zusammennehmen*
10 **It rings for ages** – *es klingelt ewig*
11 **to cause trouble** – *Stress machen*

around here. It was you who was snogging Vanessa."

Felix laughs. "Snogging? You've gone crazy! I don't know what your problem is, but I don't even know who Vanessa is. And I've got no idea why my mum said hi to me from her! Natalie, you're the one I love."

It's a pack of lies[1]. He does know Vanessa, he knows her very well, but at least he tells me that he loves me: and that's far more important than 12 seconds of making out[2] documented on a shaky old video clip on a mobile phone. I swallow and say: "OK, let's forget about all of that with Vanessa. But didn't we want to meet tonight? Aren't you coming ..."

"Sorry babe," he says, interrupting quickly, "it's not going to work tonight at all. My mum was at the shop all day and now I've got to help her keep the books[3] and tidy up the place. My Saturday is pretty much done for[4], as you can imagine. But I've got nothing to do tomorrow: how about I pick you up at half-past ten and we go to the lake? That's a good plan, right?" Before I have the chance to reply, he's already hung up.

"Leo and Vanessa may already be out of the tournament," says Mia, who I meet at the sausage stand a few minutes later, "but they're still about to score[5], I'd say." She giggles and elbows me: "Maybe I should get my phone out in case they start snogging: maybe she'll break her record with Felix?!"

"Oh, not again!" I say, shouting at her.

"Hey, what's your problem? There's me doing everything possible

....
1 **it's a pack of lies** – hier: *alles Lügen*
2 **making out** – *Knutscherei*
3 **to keep the books** – *Buchhaltung machen*
4 **done for** (Umgangssprache) – *gelaufen, im Eimer*
5 **to score** (Umgangssprache) – hier: *jdn. klarmachen*

to get them together – you could at least be grateful[1]. But maybe you should eat something first – then you'll be in a better mood. The sausages here are great in any case."

I shake my head. "No, I'm not hungry. Look, I'm sorry I was so unfriendly just now, it's just that ... everything's kind of going wrong at the moment. Felix can't come – he's got to help his mother. So all this Vanessa-and-Leo-business[2] is pretty useless. "Yeah, it's pretty bad that Felix is not there. On the other hand, the whole Vanessa-Leo-thing is good – look at it this way: those two suit each other[3] really well." "Do you mean that Leo is really in love with Vanessa?" I ask and can't stop my voice trembling[4] as I speak.

"Yes, I think so," says Mia, "but now I've got to deal with[5] the next round. We'll speak later!"

I might just as well go home now[6]. It would probably be better; after all, I'm bound to get in trouble with my mum if I don't show my face[7] sometime soon, and Mia has got to organise the tournament for the next half an hour or so. As well as that, Felix isn't coming and Leo is busy with Vanessa. I can see the pair of them at the drinks stand, laughing away[8]. My heart sinks[9] and I suddenly feel very lonely – despite the crowd. Then again, it would be rude to just disappear without telling Mia, so I make my way[10] through to her. She's at the board[11] putting up the scores.

· · · · · · · · ·

1 **grateful** – *dankbar*
2 **business** – hier: *Angelegenheit*
3 **to suit each other** – *zusammenpassen*
4 **to tremble** – *zittern*
5 **to deal with sth.** – *sich um etw. kümmern*
6 **I might just as well go home now** – *ich könnte jetzt auch genauso gut nach Hause gehen*
7 **to show one's face** – *auftauchen, sich blicken lassen*
8 **laughing away** – *lachend*
9 **my heart sinks** – *mein Herz wird schwer*
10 **to make one's way** – *sich seinen Weg bahnen*
11 **board** – *Anzeigetafel*

"Bye Mia! I'm off[1] now," I say sadly, "and don't forget to take me and Felix off the list."

"Yeah, I will. Hey, what are you doing tomorrow? We could do some English homework together and then take the dog out."

"Sorry, I can't. I'm going to the lake with Felix tomorrow," I say, "but, then again, maybe I will stop by your place. Sorry Mia, I just don't know at the moment." It's strange; just a few days ago, I would have gone crazy for the chance to spend an entire day with Felix, but now ... Suddenly, I'm just not that up for it[2] any more.

I'm already on my way home when my phone rings – it's Mia!

"Finally! I thought I wouldn't be able to get hold of you[3]. Natalie, you've got to get back here right now!"

"I'm almost home already!" I say, although it's not exactly true.

"That doesn't matter. You'll just have to come the whole way back. Seriously! Listen to this: Felix has just turned up[4] and is making a real scene[5] because he wants to play with Vanessa. It's really going crazy here – you really can't miss it[6]!"

TR. 08 In just ten minutes I'm back. It's almost dark outside, the air smells like summer and there are multi-coloured Chinese lanterns in the park. Down in the cellar of the youth centre, someone is playing the saxophone and it sounds sad. Then I see Felix and Vanessa with their arms round each other.

"Hi!" I say with emphatic coolness: "So your mum did let you come then?"

....
1 **I'm off now** (Umgangssprache) – *Ich bin dann mal weg*
2 **I'm just not that up for it** (Umgangssprache) – *Ich habe irgendwie gar keine richtige Lust*
3 **to get hold of someone** (Umgangssprache) – *jdn. (telefonisch) erwischen*
4 **to turn up** (Umgangssprache) – *antanzen, aufkreuzen*
5 **to make a real scene** – *ein Riesentheater machen*
6 **you can't miss it** – *das kannst du dir nicht entgehen lassen*

"Er ..." Felix falters[1] and pulls a face[2]. This time, though, it's not his arrogant smile. No, now he looks kind of pathetic, actually. He tries in vain[3] to get out of Vanessa's arms.

"Hm, your vocabulary[4] seems to have regressed[5] since we spoke on the phone just now!" I talk loudly so that Vanessa will hear.

"Er ... Natalie ... let me explain it to you," he says, stuttering. Then he has a go[6] at Vanessa as she starts to stroke[7] the back of his neck: "Just stop it!"

"Oh, so you can speak again now?" I say; then I turn to Vanessa.

"You know, Felix used to be able to say enough to tell me he loved me – just now, in fact, using really nice, long sentences. Then, he was even able to say that he wanted to meet me at the lake tomorrow: he knew all the words for that."

"It's all ... er ... it's all a horrible misunderstanding[8]," he says, stuttering again, "and I ... I really do have to go back to help my mum with the books. I just wanted to stop by and see what was happening here."

"You've gone absolutely crazy!" shouts Vanessa. She's very angry and, taking her arms from around his neck, steps back.

"You can't just leave! I mean, you've been telling me for days about this candle-light dinner and now Leo has just agreed to let you play the rest of the tournament in his place ... and now you're making such a scene!"

"Felix always makes a scene," I say quietly, "didn't you know that?

· · · · · · · · ·

1 **to falter** – *stolpern*
2 **to pull a face** – *das Gesicht verziehen*
3 **in vain** – *vergeblich*
4 **vocabulary** – *Wortschatz*
5 **to regress** – hier: *reduzieren*
6 **to have a go at sb.** – *jdn. anschnauzen, anfahren*
7 **to stroke** – *streicheln, kraulen*
8 **misunderstanding** – *Missverständnis*

Well, congratulations[1] Vanessa! You've really drawn first prize[2] with this guy!"

"What do you mean?" she says, looking at me uneasily.

"You'll work it out by yourself[3]," I reply. Then I turn back to Felix, who is now so fascinated[4] by his mobile phone display that you'd think[5] nothing else interesting was going on.

"And you! You can keep your declarations[6] of true love – and your trip to the lake tomorrow! I've had it up to here with you![7]"

He keeps looking at his phone. Vanessa looks at me and I get the impression that she is thinking about what I just said.

"Hm," she says after a pause, "Felix, listen: I think it's time we put an end to our relationship, too. You should go home right away – I think it's the best thing for everyone, especially you." Felix says "Pah!" and something that sounds like "stupid" and "girls" I don't quite catch it[8] though, and then he turns and goes.

I think about how I feel – am I sad? No, actually I feel good. It's like when there's been a storm[9] and the air is nice and fresh. I can think clearly again. I've got to find Mia and tell her everything.

· · · · · · · · ·

1 **congratulations** – Glückwunsch, Gratulation
2 **to draw first prize** – das große Los ziehen
3 **to work it out by oneself** (Umgangssprache) – selber drauf kommen
4 **fascinated** – fasziniert
5 **you'd think** – hier: man könnte denken
6 **declarations of true love** – Liebesschwüre
7 **I've had it up to here with you!** (Redewendung) – Ich bin so was von fertig mit dir!, Ich hab' die Schnauze voll von dir!
8 **to not quite catch sth.** – etw. nicht so genau verstehen
9 **it's like when there's been a storm** – es ist wie nach einem Gewitter

Perhaps it's fate that I come across Leo and not Mia. He's sitting on the rail that separates the youth centre from the neighbouring plot of land[1] and smiles at me as I come up to[2] him.

"Well, what do you think of my performance?" he asks. He looks

```
Love-Question 5
☑ INBOX
from Mia Mobile

Hey Nat! Did u talk
2 Felix again? What
did he say? I'm go-
ing home now so text
back! x
```

really nice, especially when he looks at me like this. It feels like I'm really noticing[3] Leo for the first time; I can feel my heart beat.

"Well then?" he repeats: "Are you satisfied, or are you annoyed because we didn't win the candle-light dinner?"

"Are you?" I ask back.

"Not one bit!" he says, shaking his head emphatically: "Ten minutes of Vanessa is really quite enough. She's completely artificial[4]; it really gets on your nerves."

"Hey, but I thought you guys were getting along fine."

"What? You're not jealous are you?"

And, suddenly, it dawns on me[5]: it would seem that boys are finally learning what girls have always known how to do[6] – make the person you like jealous. So he was in love with me the whole time! And that's why he was so shy with me the whole time and so cool with Vanessa: because he's not at all[7] interested in her.

"No, I'm not jealous; but let's not talk about Vanessa the whole evening. How about talking about us?"

· · · · · · · ·

1 **plot of land** – *Grundstück*
2 **to come up to sb.** – *sich jdm. nähern, auf jdn. zulaufen*
3 **to really notice** – *bewusst wahrnehmen*
4 **artificial** – *künstlich*
5 **it dawns on me** – *es dämmert mir*
6 **what girls have always known how to do** – hier: *was Mädchen schon immer beherrschen*
7 **not at all** – *nicht im Geringsten*

"Great idea!" he says: "I'd like to know more about you."

"OK, then let's take a nice long walk in the moonlight and I'll tell you all about my life. That's pretty romantic, don't you think?"

"Yes, it is. But are you sure you're not going to think of something better in a couple of minutes?" I have the impression that he is trying to stop himself smiling.

"I don't think I'll come up with a better idea; it's you I want," I whisper, "because I like you."

"And I like you!" He whispers back. Then he looks very serious for a second, before laughing at me: "You've won my heart[1] – and didn't even need training as a striker!"

He puts his arm around me and it feels great. With Leo nothing can go wrong: that's why I kiss him.

. . . .

1 **to win someone's heart** – *jdns. Herz im Sturm erobern*

Irene Zimmermann

Kisses, Chaos and Rides on a Sledge

"Oh no, I'm dying!" Hanna shouts this so loudly that I jump[1] and rush into[2] her room.

"Stop this rubbish[3]! I've got to do homework and I can't spend all my time looking after you," I say with all the authority that I, as the older twin sister, can muster[4] – those two minutes make all the difference. Now, what I've just said about homework isn't true, but I want peace and quiet[5] so that I can go over a few things in my mind[6]. Well, one thing in fact – what exactly did Andy mean when he said that he wanted me to write him a letter during the winter holiday? With Hanna's screaming, though, I can't think at all. My threat[7] of bringing her another pot[8] of herbal-cough tea[9] stops her for a second, but it really is only a second: Hanna has just got a text[10] from a friend of hers, and I reckon[11] it's bad news.

"Tomorrow my class has got a winter sports day! It's snowed so much recently, so they all go tobogganing[12]," she cries.

"Yes, without you," I say. I really shouldn't have said it[13], though, because now she gets a right royal[14] coughing fit. Although I'm afraid of catching something[15], I pat her back gently.

· · · · · · · · ·

1 **to jump** – hier: *zusammenzucken*
2 **to rush into somewhere** – *irgendwo hineinstürzen*
3 **Stop this rubbish!** – *Hör auf damit!*
4 **to muster** – *aufbringen*
5 **peace and quiet** (Redewendung) – *Ruhe*
6 **to go over things in one's mind** – *sich mit seinen Gedanken beschäftigen*
7 **threat** – *Drohung*
8 **(tea)pot** – *Teekanne*
9 **herbal-cough tea** – *Hustentee*
10 **text** – hier: *SMS*
11 **to reckon** (Umgangssprache) – *vermuten, denken*
12 **to toboggan** – *rodeln, Schlitten fahren*
13 **I really shouldn't have said it** – *das hätte ich mir besser verkniffen*
14 **right royal** (Umgangssprache) – *... der sich gewaschen hat*
15 **to catch sth.** – *sich anstecken, sich etw. einfangen*

She replies by gasping[1], "you just don't get it, do you?"
I'm offended[2] and about to stop my limited nursing[3] altogether[4]
and leave the room when she grabs my jumper and says that she's
suddenly had a great idea and that I can help her. When Hanna
starts talking like this, you've got to be extremely careful[5]. I'm
about to think of some excuse[6] to get out of her room when the
doorbell rings and we hear Mrs Niederegger's voice.
"Could one of you two maybe look after Lohengrin for an hour or
two?" I hear her calling up the stairs. "Perhaps you can take him
round the block quickly, too?"
I sit down next to my sister and tell her that I'll shut her mouth
by force[7] if she utters[8] even the tiniest noise. I'd much rather listen
to Hanna's coughing, sneezing and hoarseness all day than spend
just one minute with that awful wiry-haired[9] dachshund[10] with its
weak bladder[11] and continuous urge[12] to bark for hours at[13] anything
or anyone who moves a muscle[14]. Hanna grins; apart from the fact
that she's running a fever[15] of at least 39 degrees, she seems to be
healthy again.
"Marie, I've just had, like, the best idea ever[16]!" she repeats as soon
as Mrs Niederegger has stopped calling to us. "But you've got to

· · · · · · · · ·

1 **to gasp** – *röcheln*
2 **offended** – *beleidigt*
3 **nursing** – *Tätigkeit als Krankenschwester*
4 **altogether** – *gänzlich, vollständig*
5 **extremely careful** – *äußerst vorsichtig*
6 **excuse** – *Vorwand, Ausrede*
7 **by force** – *mit Gewalt*
8 **to utter** – *von sich geben*
9 **wiry-haired** – *Rauhhaar-*
10 **dachshund** – *Dackel, Dachshund*
11 **bladder** – *Blase*
12 **urge** – *Bedürfnis*
13 **to bark at sb.** – *jdn. anbellen*
14 **to move a muscle** (Redewendung) – *sich auch nur im geringsten bewegen*
15 **to run a fever** – *Fieber haben*
16 **the best idea ever** (Umgangssprache) – *eine Wahnsinnsidee*

43

promise me not to tell anyone, not a word to anyone – not even mum! Promise?"

My first instinct is to refuse, but I'm curious[1], so I nod[2]: "You can count on me[3]. But first of all I've got know what it's about, okay?"

"She looks at me for a second, then she rolls her eyes[4] and starts giggling[5] like mad[6].

"You've got no idea what's going on at the moment! I'm ... I'm so happy!" Her mobile phone beeps[7] because she's got a text-message, she takes a look at the person who's sent it[8] and then puts it under her pillow. "It's Hannes," she murmurs, "it's a message from Hannes."

"And you're in love with him?" I infer[9].

"No, not with him!" she shouts, outraged[10], "what kind of stupid idea is that? He's in my class, and you know ..."

"I know, your class is full of idiots," I say reassuringly[11] and am pleased that I don't go to the same school as Hanna. Our parents thought that twins should be given space[12] to develop independently[13] of each other and so they sent us to different schools.

Hanna nudges[14] me. Considering the fact that[15] she's been lying in bed for three days, she's still got quite a lot of strength. "You've got

. . . .

1 **curious** – *neugierig*
2 **to nod** – *nicken*
3 **to count on sb.** – *auf jdn. zählen*
4 **to roll one's eyes** – *die Augen verdrehen*
5 **to giggle** – *kichern*
6 **like a mad** – *wie verrückt, wie ein/e Irre/r*
7 **to beep** – *piepsen*
8 **person who's sent it** – *Absender*
9 **to infer** – *schlussfolgern*
10 **outraged** – *empört*
11 **reassuringly** – *beruhigend*
12 **to give sb. space** – *jdm. Freiraum geben*
13 **independently** – *unabhängig*
14 **to nudge sb.** – *jdn. anschubsen*
15 **considering the fact that** – *dafür, dass*

that funny look on your face again [1]," she says, "you're not going to get ill as well, are you? I hope not! I need your help, you see [2]."
Then she starts to tell me the whole story: it's about Maik from year nine [3], who's the only person in his class to have ticked sledging [4] on his winter sports day form. This was the reason why he was assigned [5] to Hanna's class. And when the pairs for tobogganing were being decided, he chose to ride with her. "Imagine that!" she says, and her voice sounds almost awestruck [6]: "He could have gone for [7] Nadine or Ellen, but he chose me!"
I just nod. She looks at my blank [8] face.
"You see, everyone in my class is crazy about [9] Maik," she explains, "he's such a great guy. He's so ..." – she rolls her eyes – "he's so ... well, you wouldn't get it [10], you're way too rational [11], but it's really got me bad [12]. You can't imagine how nasty Nadine and Ellen were about it. And now ..." Hanna gives me those puppy-dog eyes [13] and I actually feel sorry for her.
"Now it'll be either Nadine or Ellen with Maik on that sledge ..." I say and then put my hand on her shoulder comfortingly [14], which gets me nothing but another coughing attack [15]. "Come on Hanna, that's not all that bad. If he really likes you, then you'll get together

· · · · · · · · ·

1 **you've got that funny look on your face again** – *du guckst schon wieder so komisch*
2 **you see** – hier: *nämlich*
3 **from year nine** – *aus der neunten Klasse*
4 **sledging** – *Rodeln, Schlittenfahren*
5 **to assign** – *zuteilen*
6 **awestruck** – *ehrfürchtig*
7 **to go for** (Umgangssprache) – hier: *sich aussuchen*
8 **blank** – hier: *verständnislos*
9 **to be crazy about sb.** – *für jdn. schwärmen*
10 **to get it** – hier: *kapieren*
11 **rational** – *nüchtern*
12 **to get sb. bad** – *jdn. richtig erwischen*
13 **puppy-dog eyes** (Redewendung) – *Hundeblick*
14 **comfortingly** – *beruhigend*
15 **coughing attack** – *Hustenanfall*

– I'm certain of that."

"But we'll never see each other again – or at least not until winter sports day next year," says my twin, crying, "and you're so heartless[1] about the whole thing, Marie. Nobody's ever going to fall in love with you, believe me."

I just laugh. If only Hanna knew[2]! I'm going to write to Andy I have a totally immature[3] and horrible sister and then he will see how different I am. Perhaps he's already noticed that and has fallen in love with me? I sigh under my breath[4], but Hanna doesn't hear it anyway through her own lamentations[5].

"But I don't want to wait," shouts my twin sister, "I want to go to the winter sports ball next Saturday with Maik, you see? And you've got to help me, okay? After all, you are my bigger sister and mum's always saying that we should be able to count on one another. Then she tells me her plan.

TR. 02 "No," I reply. What I'd really like to do is to put my hand on her forehead[6] and check her temperature. I bet[7] it's gone up. "You really can't be serious![8] And anyway, my hair is a lot longer than yours and I only know Ann-Kathrin in your class. I've got absolutely no idea who is who. Everyone will notice immediately."

"But Maik won't notice. We've only seen each other a couple of

· · · · · · · · ·
1 **heartless** – *herzlos*
2 **If only Hanna knew!** – *Wenn Hanna nur wüsste!*
3 **immature** – *unreif*
4 **under one's breath** – *halblaut*
5 **lamentations** – *Gejammer*
6 **forehead** – *Stirn*
7 **to bet** – *wetten*
8 **You really can't be serious!** – *Das kann doch nicht dein Ernst sein!*

times on the playground[1]..." She takes a good look at me: "Hmm, if we put a hat on you, then nobody will notice that your hair is longer than mine. Or we could just cut it off, of course!"

I've had enough[2]. I'm just not up for[3] listening to my sister's crazy ideas. Cut off my hair? Me? She knows how proud I am of my long black hair; and I'll bet Andy likes it too! "We can't do any of that, I'm afraid," I say, "and besides[4], I've got school tomorrow. You don't expect me to bunk off school[5] do you? Now, if you want more cough-tea, just give me a shout[6]." Down in the living room, I stand in front of the window for several minutes just watching the snow. I think of Andy and his unbelievably[7] brown eyes. He's been at our table-tennis club for almost three weeks and we see each other every Tuesday and every Friday, and sometimes ... The telephone rings. Could it be Andy? Perhaps he's found out[8] my telephone number? But it's Mrs Niederegger, ringing up to complain about the huge amounts[9] of snow coming down – like there's anything I could do about it[10]!

"Oh yes, while I've got you on the phone, Lohengrin must go out today," she says, "and I'll need 50g salami and a small loaf of wholegrain bread. And while you're at it[11], you could get me a few onions ..."

· · · · · · · · ·

1 **playground** – *Pausenhof*
2 **I've had enough.** – *Mir reicht es.*
3 **to be up for sth.** – *auf etw. Lust haben*
4 **and besides** – *außerdem*
5 **to bunk off school** – *blaumachen, Schule schwänzen*
6 **just give me a shout** (Umgangssprache) – *meld' dich einfach*
7 **unbelievably** – *unglaublich*
8 **to find out** – *rausbekommen*
9 **huge amounts** – *Unmengen*
10 **like there's anything I could do about it** – *als ob ich irgendwas dafür könnte*
11 **while you're at it** (Umgangssprache) – *wo du schon dabei bist*

Resistance is futile[1], so I nod silently as our landlady[2] expands her shopping list by a good 25 further items[3].

"I'll write it all down, just in case[4]," she says by way of closing[5], "because you brought me the wrong sort of sausage last time. Lohengrin hates ring sausages, try to remember that. So, see you in five minutes?"

Hanna shouts down to me, but I can't be two places at once[6].

"Sorry, I've got to go and do Mrs Niederegger's shopping," I shout to her, grab my anorak and my hat and go running out of the flat before someone else ropes me into doing something[7]. After all, Hanna is not so ill that she won't survive if I go out for a bit[8]. Thank God[9] it's already dark outside and the snow is so thick that it is impossible to see beyond a foot or so[10]. After all, taking Lohengrin out with his red-white chequered doggy-jacket is more than just slightly[11] embarrassing. I tie him in front of the butcher's and promise him a big slice of sausage if he is quiet for once[12] before starting Mrs Niederegger's shopping. The queue in front of the sausage counter is really long, but I see a face I know[13]: it's Katharina, Andy's younger sister. What a great chance to get some information first-hand[14]! So without paying any attention[15] to the

· · · · · · · · ·

1 **resistance is futile** (Redewendung) – *Widerstand ist zwecklos*
2 **landlady** – *Vermieterin*
3 **item** – hier: *Artikel*
4 **just in case** – *vorsichtshalber*
5 **by way of closing** – *abschließend, schließlich*
6 **I can't be in two places at once** (Redewendung) – *Ich kann mich nicht zerteilen*
7 **to get roped into doing sth.** (Umgangssprache) – *gezwungen werden, etw. zu tun*
8 **for a bit** – *paar Minuten, ein Stündchen*
9 **Thank God** – *Gott sei Dank*
10 **a foot or so** – *ungefähr ein halber Meter*
11 **slightly** – *ein bisschen, leicht*
12 **for once** – *ausnahmsweise*
13 **a face I know** – *ein bekanntes Gesicht*
14 **first-hand** – *aus erster Hand*
15 **without paying any attention to sth.** – *ohne auf etw. zu achten*

older ladies' protests, I jump the queue[1] to get next to Katharina. Then I put on[2] a surprised face. "Hey! What are you doing here then?" I mumble[3] and then desperately[4] try to think of a way to move the conversation inconspicuously[5] onto her brother. I don't have to, though, because Katharina does it for me.

"Andy's just sent me a text," she says, "asking me to buy half a pound of Bologna ring sausage; he loves it."

I nod heavily and notice how suddenly quite ordinary[6] things become very interesting.

"He needs it for tomorrow, you see – I think he's going to make himself a lot of sandwiches[7]," she says, laughing, "I told him that it could be pretty hard work.[8]" I keep nodding.

"What could be pretty hard work?"

"The winter sports day: his whole class is going skiing, but Andy didn't want to go with them. After the way he fell last year, I can kind of understand it, too. So he's going to go tobogganing instead; he's in with a class from the Heine school." She doesn't get any further because the woman behind the counter[9] wants to know what she'd like: "Half a pound of Bologna ring, please," I hear her say.

"Half a pound of Bologna ring," I repeat under my breath. Then I notice that the second woman behind the counter is looking at me ready to take my order. Before I can say anything else, she's already

· · · · · · · · ·

1 **to jump the queue** – *sich vordrängeln*
2 **to put on** – hier: *aufsetzen*
3 **to mumble** – *nuscheln, murmeln*
4 **desperately** – *krampfhaft*
5 **inconspicuously** – *unauffällig*
6 **ordinary** – *alltäglich, banal*
7 **to make oneself sandwiches** – *sich ein Brot schmieren*
8 **to be pretty hard work** – *ganz schön anstrengend sein*
9 **behind the counter** – *hinter der Theke*

49

weighed[1] out the sausage, but I don't care. I'm suddenly in such a good mood that I could just hug[2] Mrs Niederegger and her dog. Without them, I wouldn't have run into[3] Katharina and wouldn't have found out that Andy is going tobogganing tomorrow. Tomorrow is winter sports day: and I'm going to be there!

I've completely forgotten Mrs Niederegger's shopping list by the time I leave the butcher's with Katharina. Somehow I'm going to have to move the topic of conversation onto Andy. Every single piece of information could be important!
"So Andy's going to be sledging[4] to-

```
Love-Question 1
☑ INBOX
from: Hanna Mobile

Hey! Where did u
go? What r u doing?
And will u go 2 the
sports day 4 me?
Love xxx
```

morrow," I say carefully, but unfortunately Katharina doesn't react at all. She is just standing there chewing her bottom lip[5].
"Damn!" she mumbles, "I forgot to get something for Sandra. Andy asked me to make sure[6] I did."
"Sandra?"
"Oh, yeah, Sandra," she says, giggling, "I think they're in love, but I don't really know. Look, I'd better go back in, otherwise[7] I'll get in trouble[8]. Andy can sometimes get really annoyed[9]."

· · · · · · · · ·
1 **to weigh** – hier: *abwiegen*
2 **to hug** – *umarmen, um den Hals fallen*
3 **to run into sb.** (Umgangssprache) – *jdn. zufällig treffen*
4 **to sledge** – *Schlitten fahren*
5 **to chew one's bottom lip** – *auf seiner Unterlippe herumkauen*
6 **Andy asked me to make sure I did** – hier: *Andy hat mich extra gebeten es zu tun.*
7 **otherwise** – *sonst*
8 **to get in trouble** – *Ärger bekommen*
9 **to get annoyed** – *sauer werden, sich aufregen*

Smash[1]! That's the sound of my Andy-dreams being shattered[2]. Who is this Sandra? Not her from table tennis? That's what I want to ask, but Katharina has already disappeared[3] into the darkness. I stand at the crossing[4] for minutes refusing[5] to believe that Andy has a girlfriend. Katharina is probably right: Andy is in love with Sandra and me, stupid as I am[6], think that he likes me. Just thinking about the fact[7] that I would have sent him a love letter during the winter holidays is enough to make me burn with embarrassment. Angrily, I slam[8] the sausage into the shopping basket; then I see Mrs Niedereggers' list and remember that she expressly[9] asked me not to buy ring sausage and that I've left Lohengrin in front of the butcher's – and then there's the rest of the shopping! Luckily, Lohengrin is still in front of the butcher's where I left him; the butcher's is now closed. It's probably a good thing that he's got a doggy-jacket with fur else he would have frozen to death[10] out here. He seems to be pretty knackered[11] when I get there; he only barks once when he sees me. I can understand how he feels – I feel the same. By way of making it up to him[12], I share[13] the sausage with him, which he – oddly enough – gulps down[14] without complaining. In the meantime, I think about how to explain to Mrs Niederegger that she won't get her shopping.

· · · · · · · · ·
1 **Smash!** – *Rums!*
2 **to shatter** – *zerschlagen, zertrümmern*
3 **to disappear** – *verschwinden*
4 **crossing** – hier: *Kreuzung*
5 **to refuse** – *sich weigern*
6 **stupid as I am** (Redewendung) – *ich blöde Kuh*
7 **just thinking about the fact that ...** – *Schon allein bei der Vorstellung, dass ...*
8 **to slam** – hier: *werfen*
9 **expressly** – *ausdrücklich*
10 **to freeze to death** – *erfrieren*
11 **knackered** (Umgangssprachlich) – *am Ende, fix und fertig*
12 **by way of making it up to him** – *als Wiedergutmachung*
13 **to share** – *teilen*
14 **to gulp down** – *verschlingen*

"I think you're falling ill[1] too," says my mother after she's parked the car in the garage, "or at least, you look like you've been in the wars[2]." She says the same to Mrs Niederegger who slinks off[3] with Lohengrin and without complaining about the missing[4] shopping. "You'd have to be blind not to see how ill you are," says my mum as she opens the door to the flat. "What does Niederegger think she's doing[5] sending you out shopping in this weather? You wouldn't even put a dog out in it!"

While I was out Hanna has got out of bed and got herself a frozen pizza. Mum frowns[6] but for once doesn't say anything about health and diet – she looks pretty beaten down[7].

"I think the best thing for both of you is to stay at home tomorrow," she says as she puts on water[8] to make tea: "I've got the early shift tomorrow, so I'll leave you to sleep in[9]."

Hanna looks horrified[10]: "But Marie is fit as a fiddle[11]", she claims[12], "she can definitely go to school."

"No, you don't know how badly I'm doing," I say, shaking my head[13]. So there! Let her think out a way[14] to sort this thing with Maik out – I've got enough problems of my own! It's during the night, about half past one, as what I have to do becomes clear to

· · · · · · · ·
1 **to fall ill** – *krank werden*
2 **to look like one has been in the wars** (Redewendung) – *einen ganz mitgenommenen Eindruck machen*
3 **to slink off** – *kleinlaut abziehen*
4 **missing** – *fehlend*
5 **What does Niederegger think she's doing ...?** – *Was fällt Niederegger bloß ein ...?*
6 **to frown** – *die Stirn runzeln*
7 **beaten down** (Umgangssprache) – *geschafft*
8 **to put water on** – *Wasser aufsetzen*
9 **to sleep in** – *ausschlafen*
10 **horrified** – *entsetzt*
11 **fit as a fiddle** – *total fit, kerngesund*
12 **to claim** – *behaupten*
13 **to shake one's head** – *den Kopf schütteln*
14 **Let her think out a way to ...** – *Soll sie doch sehen, wie sie ...*

me. I'm not just going to give Andy up! No, not me! At half past two, I wake Hanna.

"Are you nuts[1]? Do you know what time it is?" she hisses[2].

"Five to twelve", I reply, but Hanna, as always, doesn't understand. She just rolls over[3] and is asleep again within seconds. Then I pinch[4] her pretty hard and whisper in her ear: "I'll go to the sports day for you."

At this, she sits up like a bolt[5]: "Am I dreaming, or ...?"

"I'll go to the sports day for you," I repeat.

Hanna swallows and looks at me gratefully[6]. Then she hugs me emotionally[7]. "You're the best sister ever!" she says, sobbing[8]: "I'll always, always remember this."

TR. 03 It's just before six as I hear mum leave the house. Seconds later, Hanna is standing in front of me with a pile[9] of clothes under her arm and her make-up box.

"We've got to make something of you," she explains as she sees my blank look, "or do you really think that Maik will fall in love you if you look like that?"

"I thought he was supposed to fall in love with *you*," I reply, "and anyway, we're twin sisters and look completely the same." Hanna, however, isn't at all[10] impressed.

· · · · · · · · ·

1 **Are you nuts?** – *Spinnst du?*
2 **to hiss** – *zischen, fauchen*
3 **to roll over** – *sich auf die andere Seite drehen*
4 **to pinch** – *kneifen*
5 **like a bolt** – *blitzschnell*
6 **grateful** – *dankbar*
7 **emotionally** – *gerührt, emotional*
8 **to sob** – *schluchzen*
9 **a pile of** – *hier: jede Menge*
10 **not at all** – *keineswegs, kein bisschen*

"Well, I take care of my appearance[1]," she says and puts a pink turtle-neck jumper[2] and pink jeans on my bed: "What do you reckon?"

I just roll over; I hadn't imagined it like this[3]. I want to know what's going on between Andy and Sandra, and that's it. I'm not in the least intending[4] to turn up dressed as a piglet[5]. "No," I protest, as she holds up a pink scarf and matching[6] hat. "I'm not going to go about dressed like ..."

" ... a piglet!" she finishes the sentence for me: "But we're not talking about you here, we're talking about me and Maik. And he likes me in pink."

We argue[7] for a while until I finally accept my fate[8] and, with a sigh[9], put on Hanna's clothes. The only point on which I don't compromise[10] is my hair: not one centimetre less! We agree that I'll put my hair up[11] and put on a pink hat. Since I look pretty pale[12] in her pink scarf, I don't protest as she gets to work with the make-up box.

"I'll do you up[13] as an ice-princess or snow-queen or something like that," she murmurs[14] as she mixes up various colours: "Maik is going to go weak at the knees[15] when he sees you. You've got to make

· · · · · · · · ·

1 **I take care of my appearance** – *ich mache was aus meinem Typ*
2 **turtle-neck jumper** – *Rollkragenpullover*
3 **I hadn't imagined it like this.** – *So hatte ich mir das nicht vorgestellt.*
4 **I'm not in the least intending to ...** – *Ich habe nicht die geringste Absicht ...*
5 **piglet** – *Schweinchen*
6 **matching** – hier: *passend*
7 **to argue** – hier: *herumdiskutieren*
8 **to accept one's fate** – *sich seinem Schicksal fügen*
9 **with a sigh** – *seufzend*
10 **the only point on which I don't compromise** – *der einzige Punkt, bei dem ich hart bleibe*
11 **to put up one's hair** – *seine Haare hochstecken*
12 **pale** – *blass*
13 **to do sb. up** (Umgangssprache) – *jdn. aufmotzen, aufbrezeln*
14 **to murmur** – *murmeln*
15 **to go weak at the knees** – *weiche Knie bekommen*

sure you[1] get him to agree to go to the winter sports ball with me
– got that?[2] He's got to be, like, totally in love with me ... Damn it,
keep still while I'm doing your eyelids!" She cleans off my eyelids
with cotton and then starts afresh[3]. "Look at that," she says as she
finishes off and checks my face, her head tilted to the side[4], "you
look really pretty!"

As Hanna goes out to go and get hairspray from mum's room I
take a deep breath[5] and decide to risk[6] a look in the mirror. As it
happens[7], I'm relatively impressed: I really don't look like normal
Marie anymore, although I don't look like normal Hanna either.
As I tell Hanna this, she just laughs.

"Maik will definitely recognise you, don't worry. He'll see how
Hanna looks even prettier than he thought. Now, don't breathe for
a second." Then she covers me and the room in a fog[8] of hairspray
and then gets a terrible coughing fit. "I've lain out some breakfast
for you in the kitchen," she pants[9] after a while, "but I'm back off
to bed now. Somehow I still don't feel that good." Hanna is sometimes unbearable[10], but she can be really nice, too. I'm touched[11] as I
look at the kitchen table: there's a cup of cocoa, chocolate cookies
and two muesli bars. She's even made me a sandwich to take with
me. It's very sweet of her, but I'm not at all hungry at the moment;
I don't know what I'm going to do, either.

· · · · · · · · ·

1 **you've got to make sure you ...** – *du musst unbedingt ...*
2 **Got that?** (Umgangssprache) – *Haste gehört?*
3 **to start afresh** – *neu anfangen*
4 **head tilted to the side** – *mit schrägem Kopf*
5 **to take a deep breath** – *tief durchatmen*
6 **to risk** – *riskieren*
7 **as it happens** – *in der Tat*
8 **fog** – *Nebel*
9 **to pant** – *hervorstoßen*
10 **unbearable** – *unerträglich, unmöglich*
11 **touched** – *gerührt*

The idea seemed simple last night: show up[1] at the winter sports day and then get Andy to realise that it's me he really loves. In the cold light of day[2], this seems completely absurd. While I'm at it, I'm supposed to get Maik to fall in love with me, too. A sledge! I need a sledge, too, I suddenly remember. When I ask Hanna for one though, she just laughs and tells me not even to think about[3] bringing my own sledge. After all, my job is to spend all day with Maik on his sledge. I nod and go back into the kitchen.

"You should get going[4]!" shouts Hanna: "If you've got any questions, just ask Ann-Kathrin – I've told her everything. Got it?"

"Yes!" I shout into the bedroom and, since my sister will be at home all day, take my dark-blue anorak out of the wardrobe instead of her fluffy[5] white coat. I want to have at least one thing of mine on[6]. Hanna, however, seems to have a sixth sense[7]: barefoot[8] and still wearing her pyjamas, she runs down the stairs after me with her white fluffy coat.

"I can't go sledging with that – it's completely impractical[9]. Look, I've got your clothes on, have your rucksack on my back and have your makeup on my face: that really is more than enough[10], don't you think?" I say quickly. "And anyway, I really have to get a move on[11] – the bus will be here in three minutes." Hanna has no choice other than[12] to go back inside. It won't do her any harm to realise

· · · · · · · · ·

1 **to show up** (Umgangssprache) – *aufkreuzen*
2 **in the cold light of day** – *bei Tageslicht betrachtet*
3 **not to even think about doing sth.** (Redewendung) – *nicht einmal daran denken, etw. zu tun*
4 **you should get going** – *du musst los*
5 **fluffy** – *Plüsch-*
6 **to have on** – *tragen (Kleidung)*
7 **sixth sense** – *sechster Sinn*
8 **barefoot** – *barfuß*
9 **impractical** – *unpraktisch*
10 **that really is more than enough** – *das reicht jetzt wirklich*
11 **to get a move on** (Umgangssprache) – *sich ranhalten*
12 **Hanna has no choice other than to ...** – *Hanna bleibt nichts anderes übrig, als ...*

that she can't always have her way[1], I think as I run to the bus stop.

TR. 04   I know the Heine school a little bit because Hanna's in the drama club[2] there and I've gone to all the performances[3], of course. So I walk up to the main entrance[4] and I'm pretty relieved to see a group of people with sledges. They can only be Hanna's classmates[5]! Thank God no-one can hear my heart beating as I approach.

"Oh, hey Hanna," says one girl and stands next to me, "I forgot that CD – really sorry about that. You're not upset, are you?" Suddenly[6], I'm feeling a lot better – I must really look like Hanna. "No, don't worry about it," I say coolly[7] and look around inconspicuously for Ann-Kathrin, Hanna's best friend. But as much as I look around for her, I just can't see her.

And of all the guys who sit on the wall in front of the main building, which one could be Maik? "He's the one who just looks fantastic," my sister had told me, but they all look pretty average[8] to me. They're all just sitting there in their big winter jackets. Then again, *I* don't have to fall in love with *Maik*. An

```
Love-Question 2
☑ INBOX
from: Hanna Mobile

Hey Sis! Why didn't
u eat ur breakfast?
Did u get the bus? Do
people think ur me?
;-)
```

· · · · · · · · ·

1 **to have one's way** – *sich durchsetzen*
2 **drama club** – *Theaterclub*
3 **performance** – *Aufführung*
4 **main entrance** – *Haupteingang*
5 **classmates** – *Klassenkamaraden*
6 **suddenly** – *plötzlich, schlagartig*
7 **coolly** – *lässig*
8 **average** – *durchschnittlich, nichtssagend*

older woman wearing a thick woollen sweater with matching mittens[1] walks up to us[2]. This can be no-body but Mrs Schlotterbeck, the sports teacher.

"All the sledges have been put away[3], and the bus will be here any moment," she explains, "so can we just quickly count who's here?" She takes off her mittens and does a quick count. "Right, 27 – who's missing?"

"Ann-Kathrin," shouts a girl with a red hat, "she sent me a text – her dad's car's broken down[4]."

Mrs Schlotterbeck just shakes her head. She's about to[5] say something, but then the bus comes by and since it is not allowed to stop in front of the school, we all have to get straight in.

The driver is pretty annoyed as it is[6] and so when Mrs Schlotterbeck says we have to wait for another pupil, he shakes his head very decisively[7]. "We leave at 7:30," he shouts into the microphone. "If she isn't there by then, that's just too bad.[8]" With that[9], he drives us onto the road.

I sink onto the seat behind the driver. This really is the last thing I need[10] – without Ann-Kathrin, I'm pretty helpless. How am I supposed to know who Maik is, for example? I try to remember a few names from Hanna's class: I manage to[11] think of Nadine, Ellen and Jonas, but that doesn't help because I've got no idea who they

· · · · · · · · ·

1 **mittens** – *Fäustlinge*
2 **to walk up to sb.** – *jdm. entgegenkommen*
3 **to put away** – *verstauen*
4 **to break down** – *eine Panne haben*
5 **to be about to do sth.** – *kurz davor sein, etw. zu tun*
6 **as it is** – *auch so schon*
7 **decisively** – *entschieden*
8 **That's just too bad!** (Redewendung) – *Pech geabt!*
9 **with that** – *darauf hin*
10 **This really is the last thing I need.** (Redewendung) – *Das hat mir gerade noch gefehlt.*
11 **to manage to do sth.** – *es schaffen, etw. zu tun*

are. What I'd really like to do is to just forget the whole thing, but now we're on the motorway and I realise that I'm going to have to spend the next ten hours in this class. Besides that, I've got to look out for number one here[1]. If I understood Katharina correctly, we're meeting the skiers on the mountain and that's when Andy will be joining our group.

"I'll just sit down next to you," I hear and Mrs Schlotterbeck falls into the seat next to me with a loud sigh: "This is the last time I do winter sports day!" she says and looks me up and down[2].

"Er, Hanna: you did know we were going tobogganing and not dancing at the disco, right?"

I go red and mumble something; Mrs Schlotterbeck shakes her head. I'd really like to go and wash this black eyeliner[3] straight off, but because I'm afraid that everything will only end up looking worse, I don't.

"Sandra, chuck[4] me the CD would you?" I hear someone say and immediately infer that this must be Andy's Sandra. I stand up and take a look back down the bus; a blonde girl is throwing the CD to a boy. What I'd really like to do is to stand up and go and talk to her about Andy, but of course I can't. Besides that, a mobile phone starts ringing and Mrs Schlotterbeck jumps up[5] to tell us that she will be collecting all phones for safekeeping[6].

"Sandra, that means you too[7]!" she shouts over to a chubby[8] dark-haired girl who tries to put her phone into her rucksack. So there's

. . . .

1 **to look out for number one.** (Redewendung) – *sich auf seine eigenen Interessen konzentrieren.*
2 **to look sb. up and down** – *jdn. mustern*
3 **eyeliner** – *Lidstrich*
4 **to chuck** (Umgangssprache) – *werfen, schmeißen*
5 **to jump up** – *aufspringen, losspurten*
6 **for safekeeping** – hier: *um sie aufzubewahren*
7 **that mean's you too** – *das gilt auch für dich*
8 **chubby** – *pummelig*

another Sandra – and a big problem! Hanna and I had agreed that I would ring her in case of an emergency[1], but that option is gone now, too. Mrs Schlotterbeck is standing right in front of me, holding out her hand with a strict[2] face:

"Hanna, your phone please, anytime today'll do[3]!" So I've now got no other option than to give her my mobile. While all this was happening[4], we've left the motorway and are driving up a mountain road with lots of bends[5] and I suddenly feel very ill. Maybe it's not the road, though; perhaps it's that I haven't had any breakfast, or that I realise what an awkward situation[6] I've got myself into. Well, not me, but Hanna, I think to myself and get angry. I decide never again to let myself be influenced by my sister. Let her think out a way to get with Maik. And as for Andy – has he lost it completely?[7] I mean, asking me to write him a letter, looking at me as if he's in love with me and all the while[8] having Sandra as a girlfriend! This anger seems to do me good[9] and I don't feel ill anymore. Anyway, we're now at the car park on the mountain and I can see a horde[10] of skiers: and Andy is right in the middle of them. Andy: this boy looks like every girl's dream boyfriend. Just for a second, I feel slightly uneasy[11], but then I get a grip of myself[12]. I'm just pretty excited to see what Andy will do when he sees me; or did I tell him that I have a twin sister? I don't think I did!

· · · · · · · · ·

1 **in case of emergency** – *im Notfall*
2 **strict** – *streng*
3 **anytime today'll do** (Redewendung) – *wenn's geht, heute noch*
4 **while all this was happening** – *inzwischen*
5 **bend** – *Kurve*
6 **awkward situation** – *blöde Situation*
7 **Has he lost it completely?** (Redewendung) – *Was glaubt er eigentlich?*
8 **all the while** – *die ganze Zeit*
9 **to do sb. good** – *jdm. guttun*
10 **horde** – *Horde*
11 **uneasy** – *flau, unsicher*
12 **to get a grip of oneself** – *sich wieder fassen*

"So, go get your sledges, then your partners, and then off you go![1]" shouts Mrs Schlotterbeck, emphasising[2] her words by blowing her whistle[3]: "See you back here in two hours for the snow picnic. Now, onwards[4]!"

I do everything as slowly as I can; after all, I still don't have the foggiest[5] who my partner Maik is. Mrs Schlotterbeck asks me what the matter is[6] and I just mumble something about feeling ill after the journey. Two girls who are standing around indecisively[7] in the gangway[8] nod and agree that the bus driver was awful and drove like a racing-driver who missed his calling[9]. In the meantime[10], most of the class have got their sledges and are running off. The one left behind is bound to be Maik, I conclude[11] and wait with Hanna's rucksack. Anyway, I don't want to end up meeting Andy too early, either. I take a careful look out of the window – perhaps he's stood next to Sandra and has his arm around her – but that's when he sees me looking at him. He looks up at me, completely disbelieving[12]. Before you know it[13], he's in the bus talking to me. "Marie?"

I'm about to nod, but then I remember, thank God, that I'm Hanna today and shake my head. "Hanna," I say and can't help the fact that my question gets stuck in my throat[14].

· · · · · · · · ·

1 **Off you go!** – *Und los!*
2 **to emphasise** – *betonen, unterstreichen*
3 **whistle** – *Schiedsrichterpfeife*
4 **onwards!** – *vorwärts!*
5 **to not have the foggiest** (Umgangssprache) – *keinen blassen Schimmer haben*
6 **... what the matter is** (Redewendung) – *was ist los ist.*
7 **indecisively** – *unschlüssig*
8 **gangway** – *Mittelgang*
9 **to miss one's calling** – *seine Berufung verfehlen*
10 **in the meantime** – *in der Zwischenzeit*
11 **to conclude** – *schlussfolgern*
12 **disbelieving** – *ungläubig*
13 **before you know it** – *im Handumdrehen, ruck, zuck*
14 **to get stuck in one's throat** – *im Hals stecken bleiben*

"Oh come on![1] Are you kidding me?[2] he says, "you look like Marie, you talk like Marie …"

"You've got me mixed up[3]," I laugh, "my twin-sister is called Marie, but I'm Hanna! And why don't you tell me who you are?"

Now Mrs Schlotterbeck has discovered us: "What's going on here?[4] Are you two deaf[5] or something? The bus is about to be locked up, so get out into the fresh air and snow!"

Andy smiles at me and suddenly I feel completely different towards him. What I'd really like to do is to hug him and then take him tobogganing all day. Seconds later, however, I'm pleased I didn't do that because this chubby Sandra girl comes up to us[6] and beams at[7] Andy.

"I've been waiting for you," she says and kisses him on the cheek.

For a second it looks as if he finds this unpleasant[8], but then I see how he puts his arm around her and my first urge is to punch[9] him. Has he lost it completely? Does he think he's irresistible[10]? The way he was smiling at me just as couple of seconds ago; and now he's doing the same with fatty[11] here! I turn to the side and pretend to be as disinterested[12] as possible; so let them have a bit of a snog[13] if that's what they want to do[14]. Whatever the case, Andy is

· · · · · · · · ·

1 **Oh come on!** – *Ach komm schon!*
2 **Are you kidding me?** – *Willst du mich reinlegen?*
3 **You've got me mixed up.** – *Du verwechselt mich.*
4 **What's going on here?** – *Was ist denn hier los?*
5 **deaf** – *taub*
6 **to come up to sb.** – *auf jdn. zukommen*
7 **to beam at sb.** – *jdn. anstrahlen*
8 **unpleasant** – *unangenehm*
9 **to punch sb.** – *jdm. eine runterhauen*
10 **irresistable** – *unwiderstehlich*
11 **fatty** (Umgangssprache) – *Dickerchen, Pummelchen*
12 **disinterested** – *desinteressiert*
13 **to have a bit of a snog** (Umgangssprache) – *rumknutschen*
14 **if that's what they want to do** – *wenn ihnen danach zumute ist*

dead as far as I'm concerned[1]. Well, at least as long as he's snogging this Sandra girl! From now on, I decide, I'm going to be a good person and concentrate on making my sister's love story happen. I'm going to concentrate on Maik. With this in mind, I head towards[2] the boy who is sitting around on his sledge looking lost; Andy shouts something after me, but I decide not to turn around.

TR. 05 "Hi!" I say to Maik and size him up[3]. Dark hair, dark eyes, a couple of pimples[4] on his chin; OK, so he's not exactly my type, but *I* don't have to fall in love with him. Hanna does always have slightly odd tastes[5]. Maik has got up and his fiddling around with[6] the strap[7] on the sledge, somehow tying it around his right hand. I look at him, amused because, even after two minutes, he hasn't quite managed to get free of it[8].
"Thanks", he mumbles, turning slightly red.
I beam at him and ask: "Shall we?[9]"
He turns even redder. My inner voice[10] tells me that he's completely in love with Hanna as it is and that I don't have to do anything else; but because I'm so cool about this kind of stuff[11], I decide to flirt with him shamelessly[12]. We fight our way uphill[13] through the snow. Andy and Sara are behind us and I can hear his voice,

· · · · · · · · ·

1 **as far as I'm concerned** – *für mich*
2 **to head towards sb.** – *auf jdn. zusteuern*
3 **to size sb. up** – *jdn. mustern*
4 **pimple** – *Pickel(chen)*
5 **slightly odd taste** – *etwas merkwürdiger Geschmack*
6 **to fiddle around with sth.** – *mit etw. herumfummeln*
7 **strap** – *Schnur*
8 **to get free of sth.** – *sich von etw. befreien*
9 **Shall we?** – *Wollen wir?*
10 **inner voice** – *innere Stimme*
11 **cool about this kind of stuff** – hier: *so locker*
12 **shamelessly** – hier: *hemmungslos*
13 **uphill** – *bergaufwärts*

although I can't hear what he's saying.

Maik looks at me: "Can you go any further?" he asks. He sounds concerned[1]: "I can pull[2] you up if you can't."

Of course I can go further, I want to say. After all, I'm in the table tennis club and do regular circuit training[3] there, but I stop myself. Instead, I smile gratefully and sit on the sledge. In the meantime Andy and Sandra have drawn ahead of us; she looks over at me jealously[4] and, a few minutes later[5], she's sat on the sledge and Andy is pulling. Serves him right[6], I think without a shred of pity[7]: it's only right that Sandra is so fat. She weighs at least ten or fifteen kilos more than me and Andy must be having a pretty hard time.

Maik turns round: "You OK?" he asks. As I look at him blankly, he just laughs out loud[8].

"Oh yeah, I'm fine!" I say. "And you're doing a great job!" Andy, however, isn't doing so well. It looks like having Sandra on the sled is testing his fitness to the limit[9]. We're about to overtake[10] them without even trying[11].

"Hanna! Watch out!" shouts a voice. It takes me a second to work out[12] that I'm meant by that – and just as I realise this, the snowball hits me – straight in the face! I hear someone shout – then I notice that it's me. Maik is standing in front of me, looking horrified; and there's a girl and a boy running towards us.

· · · · · · · · ·

1 **concerned** – besorgt
2 **to pull** – ziehen
3 **cicuit training** – Zirkeltraining
4 **jealously** – neidisch
5 **a few minutes later** – kurze Zeit später
6 **Serves him right!** – Geschieht ihm recht!
7 **without a shred of pity** – ohne eine Spur von Mitleid
8 **to laugh out loud** – laut lachen
9 **to test sb.'s fitness to the limit** – jdm. alles abverlangen
10 **to overtake** – überholen
11 **without even trying** – locker, mit links
12 **to work out** – hier: kapieren

"Lars, you're such an idiot!" shouts the girl.

I'd really like to agree to this by nodding, but I don't dare[1] because it feels as if my nose might just fall off of my face. Maik has knelt down[2] and is dabbing[3] at my face with a tissue. It really hurts and I try as hard as I can not to cry; especially since Andy is standing there – not right next to me, but there nonetheless[4]. He could take my arm and comfort[5] me, I think; then I remember that he thinks that I'm my sister. I try to smile and then I notice just how badly my nose is bleeding[6].

"We'll be fine[7]," murmurs Maik and takes out another tissue, "just try leaning your head back[8]." He puts his rucksack up against my back and asks Andy to hold the tissue for second.

"I can't," says Andy, "I'm sorry. I can deal with[9] karate fighters if you like, but I can't handle blood, I'm afraid. Sorry!" He grabs Sandra's arm[10] and goes off.

"Coward!" I hiss through my teeth, but it comes out somewhat unclearly and Maik just says that I should keep still.

The boy who hit me with the snowball has made sure[11] I'm still alive:"Next time just make sure you get out of the trajectory[12]," he says by way of advice[13] and then throws another snowball at someone else; I hope it's Mrs Schlotterbeck and that he gets in real

· · · · · · · · ·

1 **to not dare to do sth.** – *sich etw. nicht trauen*
2 **to kneel down** – *sich herunterbeugen*
3 **to dab** – *tupfen*
4 **nonetheless** – *immerhin*
5 **to comfort sb.** – *jdn. trösten*
6 **to bleed** – *bluten*
7 **We'll be fine** – *Das haben wir gleich*
8 **to lean one's head back** – *den Kopf nach hinten zu legen*
9 **to deal with sth./sb.** – *es mit jdm./etw. aufnehmen*
10 **to grab sb.'s arm** – *jdn. am Arm packen*
11 **to make sure** – hier: *sich überzeugen*
12 **trajectory** – *Flugbahn*
13 **to say by way of advice** – *raten*

trouble[1]. I'm no longer bleeding and I touch my nose carefully. My nose seems fine, except that it feels huge.

"You took a real smack there[2]!" says Maik: "You're swelling up[3] a bit."

"What, my whole face?" I ask, horrified.

He looks at me. "Your nose and eyes definitely," he says, "so maybe we should put some snow on it. I've heard that you should keep swollen areas cool."

"God no![4]" I shout, horrified again as I see him with a handful[5] of snow: "To be honest, I can't stand the idea of any more snow[6] right now." Maik laughs and sits down next to me on the sledge. He takes a bar of chocolate out of his back-pack and shares it with me. I'm happy that Lars hasn't smacked one of my teeth out. In the meantime, the toboggan run[7] has become pretty full; I can see Sandra hanging onto[8] Andy in a pretty theatrical way. Lars is still chucking snowballs. Just for a moment, I wish he'd get[9] Sandra with one. Then Andy would run off because he can't stand the sight of[10] blood, and then … I must have sighed pretty loud because Maik looks at me, worried.

"Does it still hurt badly?" he asks: "Shall I go and get some painkillers[11] from Mrs Schlotterbeck?"

At first, I say "No". Then I notice that Andy and Sandra are stand-

• • • • • • • • •

1 **to get in real trouble** – *gewaltigen Ärger kriegen*
2 **You took a real smack there.** – *Da hast du einen heftigen Schlag abbekommen.*
3 **to swell up** – *zuschwellen*
4 **God no!** – *Bloß nicht!*
5 **handful** – *eine Handvoll*
6 **I can't stand the idea of any more snow.** – *Ich kann keinen Schnee mehr sehen.*
7 **toboggan run** – *Rodelbahn*
8 **to hang onto sb.** – *sich an jdm. festklammern*
9 **to get** – hier: *treffen, erwischen*
10 **to not be able to stand the sight of sth.** – *etw. nicht sehen können*
11 **painkiller** – *Schmerztablette*

ing next to her. Andy should see how badly I'm doing – after all, he thinks I'm Marie's sister, so he really should be making a bit more of a show[1] than he is now. "That's probably not a bad idea," I say, "would you mind[2]?"

Maik nods and runs off to Mrs Schlotterbeck, who is over on the toboggan run. I use this time to take a quick look in the handmirror[3] in Hanna's rucksack; after all, I want to see what I look like after that snowball-attack.

"Oh dear!" says Mrs Schlotterbeck: "You look bad." For once, she's absolutely right. Maik and her are both bent over me and look, worried[4]. I just nod – there really is nothing to say right now. The shock of my swollen face and the dried[5] blood is still pretty heavy. I remember that I've got table-tennis training the day after tomorrow – the last time before the Christmas holidays – and Andy will be flabberghasted[6] when he sees me. This kind of thing can't be covered up by all the make-up in the world! Anyway, I say to myself, it's not a problem: now that Andy has Sandra, I never need to go to the table-tennis club ever again.

"Can you hear me?" asks Mrs Schlotterbeck, waving[7] her thick mittens about in front of my face: "What a shame that we've left all the phones in the bus. If we hadn't, we could call for help now."

"Should I run down to the bus?" asks Maik.

"The bus is gone – we're being picked up at three thirty."

· · · · · · · · ·

1 **He really should be making more a show.** – hier: *Er hätte schon ein bisschen mehr Anteilnahme zeigen können.*
2 **Would you mind?** – *Bist du so lieb?*
3 **handmirror** – *Kosmetikspiegel*
4 **worried** – *bekümmert*
5 **dried** – *getrocknet*
6 **to be flabberghasted** – *aus allen Wolken fallen*
7 **to wave sth. about** – *mit etw. herumfuchteln*

"It's fine," I say with a weary smile[1]. As I do, a shrill[2] shout sounds[3] up from the toboggan run and Mrs Schlotterbeck runs off to quieten things down[4]. Maik is now sitting down next to me.

"She doesn't have any painkillers. But you can go ahead and[5] finish the chocolate. I read somewhere that it's supposed to dull pain[6].

This Maik guy is really nice. He might not be my type, but I can see why my sister has fallen in love with him. He rearranges[7] the rucksacks so that I can lean back comfortably. It begins to snow, so he pushes the sledge under a fir tree[8] and we sit there watching the snow fall, eating sausage sandwiches and muesli bars, followed by Christmas biscuits. As he notices that I'm getting cold[9], he wraps[10] his thick scarf around me and I take this opportunity to move a bit closer to[11] him. He looks at me so nicely that I'd love to just kiss him on the cheek[12]. Thankfully, I remember that I'm only here as a deputy[13] and move away slightly. Hanna should count herself lucky she's got me as a sister[14]: anyone else would have bagged[15] Maik, I'm pretty sure of that. He's just such a cutie[16]. Those little spots on his chin don't change that and you can wash those off anyway.

"Shall we sledge for a bit[17] then?" he asks: "Otherwise you're just

· · · · · · · · ·

1 **weary** – *matt, schwach, flau*
2 **shrill** – *schrill, gellend*
3 **to sound** – *ertönen*
4 **to quieten things down** – *für Ruhe zu sorgen*
5 **you can go ahead and …** – *du kannst ruhig*
6 **to dull pain** – *schmerzlindernd wirken*
7 **to rearrange** – *zurechtrücken*
8 **fir tree** – *Tannenbaum*
9 **to get cold** – *frieren*
10 **to wrap** – *wickeln*
11 **to move a bit closer to sb.** – *an jdn. heranrücken*
12 **on the cheek** – *auf die Wange*
13 **as a deputy** – *vertretungsweise*
14 **Hanna should count herself lucky she's got me as a sister.** – *Hanna kann von Glück reden, dass ich ihre Schwester bin.*
15 **to bag sth.** (Umgangssprache) – *sich etw. unter den Nagel reißen*
16 **he's a cutie** – *er ist ein Süßer*
17 **for a bit** (Umgangssprache) – *eine Runde, ein bisschen*

going to get colder and colder. Or would you rather ..."

"Good idea," I reply quickly. Although I'm actually more warm than anything at the moment, I think it's better for us to be with the others.

"We'll go very slowly, too, so you've got nothing to worry about[1]," he says and takes my hand has go the last few meters up to the top of the hill. We're about to set off[2] as I see Andy – without Sandra. I've got to use this moment, so I pretend[3] that my bootlaces[4] have come undone[5] and Andy comes up to us. 'Pull yourself together[6] and smile', I think to myself and, although it hurts to smile, I do it: you've got to suffer to be beautiful[7]. He smiles his 'Andy-smile' back and I notice that I'm starting to melt[8].

"You could star in a horror film, you know," he shouts, "you wouldn't need any make-up!"

I shut my mouth. What I'd really like to do now is to start an avalanche[9] or do anything that will cause Andy to disappear forever. While I'm thinking this, however, he's already turned round and is waving at Sandra as she pulls up her sledge.

"Don't take it personally," says Maik, "you'll look perfectly fine by the winter sports ball!"

The words "winter sports ball" flash through my mind – Hanna wanted me to ... "Shall we go together?" I ask, pretty directly. He looks at me and glows[10].

· · · · · · · · ·

1 **you've got nothing to worry about** – *du brauchst keine Angst zu haben*
2 **to set off** – *losfahren*
3 **to pretend** – *so tun, also ob*
4 **bootlaces** – *Schnürsenkel*
5 **to come undone** – *aufgehen*
6 **to pull oneself together** – *sich zusammenreißen*
7 **You've got to suffer to be beautiful.** – *Wer schön sein will muss leiden.*
8 **to melt** – *schmelzen, dahinschmelzen*
9 **to start an avalanche** – *eine Lawine lostreten*
10 **to glow** – *glühen*

"Are you sure?" he asks. I nod – of course I'm sure! Well, Hanna is." OK, it's just it's a bit of a surprise," he says quietly, "because I always thought you didn't really notice me[1], you know ..." He looks at me, makes a kind of vague[2] movement with his hand and, as he does, he looks so cute that I could almost cry.

"I always thought *you* didn't notice *me*," I reply. His face is right next to mine. I hear Mrs Schlotterbeck's loud voice as she shouts at[3] someone – hopefully at that Lars guy – but it doesn't matter now anyway. I slowly move towards Maik and kiss him lightly on the cheek. Then we sledge down the toboggan run. Hanna can be satisfied with[4] my performance[5].

TR. 06 On the way back, Maik sits next to me. Lars has said sorry to me, but only because Mrs Schlotterbeck forced him to. Andy is somewhere on the bus too – at the back with Sandra – but I don't care about that. Maik and I don't talk much. From time to time he looks at me as if he can't believe his luck[6]; I smile back at him. Although smiling is difficult: firstly, my face hurts and secondly ... I'd kind of like someone like Maik for myself. Shame he doesn't have a twin brother. The bus is struggling through[7] the evening rush-hour[8] and it's about half past five when we get back to the school. Mrs Schlotterbeck gives us our mobile phones back and I see that Hanna has tried to call me at least five times. At first, I want to call her to let her know that everything is

· · · · · · · · ·

1 **to not really notice sb.** – *jdn. nicht so richtig wahrnehmen*
2 **vague** – *vag*
3 **to shout at sb.** – *jdn. anbrüllen*
4 **to be satisfied with sth.** – *mit etw. zufrieden sein*
5 **performance** – *Leistung*
6 **as if he can't believe his luck** – *als ob er sein Glück nicht fassen kann*
7 **to struggle through sth.** – *sich durch etw. quälen*
8 **evening rush-hour** – *Feierabendverkehr*

fine, but since Maik offers to take me home, I decide to wait with the good news.

"I think I'll stay at home for a few days; well, at least until my face has gone down[1]," I say as we turn into my street. I just manage to remember that Hanna really is quite ill.

"And what about the winter sports ball? Hanna, I really want to go with you ..."

```
Love-Question 3
☑ INBOX
from: Hanna Mobile

R u there? Why rn't u
picking up the phone?
Is everything
alright?
Love, Hanna xxx
```

"I'll be fine by then!" I say quickly and because we're running across the road, he takes my hand and doesn't let go[2]. I'm not sure that Hanna wanted me to hold hands with him for this long, or kiss him in front of the front door. After all, she could be behind the curtains[3] looking at us.

"I'm really cold," I say, which isn't a lie[4]. I really am trembling, although I don't know how much that has to do with cold, "I've got to go inside."

He gives me my things – which he had packed into his rucksack so that I didn't have to carry a heavy bag – and is about to say something, but I shut the door very quickly and take a deep breath. The first thing I notice as I hang up[5] my anorak in the wardrobe and take off my boots, is that the kitchen is in complete chaos. The

. . . .

1 **to go down** – hier: *abschwellen*
2 **to let go** - *loslassen*
3 **behind the curtains** - *hinter der Gardine*
4 **which isn't a lie** - *was nicht gelogen ist*
5 **to hang up** - *aufhängen*

door is ajar[1], revealing[2] a scene of total devastation[3]. Somebody must have tried to make a pizza, I suspect[4] as I see the remains[5] on the oven tray. It all looks pretty unprofessional, though, so I'm guessing that it's Hanna. Perhaps she suddenly got a craving[6] for some food. On the way up to her room I see the light on the answering machine[7] blinking and listen to the messages: one person has dialled the wrong number and our mum has told us that she's stopping by[8] a friend's house after work and won't be back until about half-past nine. Well, at least that gives my sister enough time to tidy up[9] the kitchen. I knock on her door, but there's no reaction. I knock again, then I open the door. No trace of Hanna[10]! It takes a few minutes for me to work out that Hanna must have left the house. Her coat and boots are missing in any case[11]. Her mobile phone isn't where it normally is either. I start to panic; looking at the kitchen, it would seem that she left in quite a hurry[12]. And why did she keep trying to ring me? Something must have happened! I just hope that it's not serious. Hanna, pretty ill, tries to call me and then uses her remaining strength[13] to drag[14] herself to the doctors? No, that can't be it, because she must have used her makeup and changed clothes several times – you can see that by

· · · · · · · · ·

1 **ajar** – *angelehnt*
2 **revealing** – *den Blick freigebend auf*
3 **devastation** – *Verwüstung*
4 **to suspect** – *mutmaßen*
5 **remains** – *Reste*
6 **to get a craving for sth.** – *Heißhunger auf etw. bekommen*
7 **answering machine** – *Anrufbeantworter*
8 **to stop by at sb.'s** – *bei jdm. vorbeischauen*
9 **to tidy up** – *wieder in Ordnung bringen*
10 **no trace of Hanna** – *von Hanna keine Spur*
11 **in any case** – *jedenfalls*
12 **in quite a hurry** – *in ziemlicher Eile*
13 **remaining strength** – *letzte Kraft*
14 **to drag oneself** – *sich schleppen*

the clothes strewn[1] across the bathroom. So what happened then? I call her mobile number, but of course I only get her voicemail[2]. Should I tell mum? No, she'll just get angry. Or perhaps I should call dad. No, he's in Italy on business[3] and so there's nothing he can do anyway. What I'd really like to do now is to call Maik, but I can't do that, of course. So I decide to ring Mrs Niederegger's doorbell and ask a few careful[4] questions. She must know something. As I'm in the stairwell[5], I hear the front door being opened and a voice humming[6]. I know that voice – it can only be Hanna.

TR. 07 "What have you been doing?" I shout down, so loud that Mrs Niederegger opens the door and says that it's just past seven and that we're making too much noise. She then asks if I'd do her shopping for her tomorrow. "Of course," I call up to her, slightly more quietly and, before she can say anything else, I come running up the stairs with Hanna.
"Wow, what a day!"
"Yes," I reply and take a look at her. She looks completely fit and healthy.
"Yes," I repeat, "I'm sure it was quite a day; but do you mind explaining to me where you've been? You're written off sick[7] and should be in bed. That's why ..."
"Marie! I'm the happiest person alive[8]!" She hugs me and dances

· · · · · · · · ·
1 **strewn** – *verstreut*
2 **voicemail** – *Mailbox*
3 **on business** – *für die Firma, dienstlich*
4 **careful** – *vorsichtig*
5 **stairwell** – *Treppenhaus*
6 **to hum** – *summen*
7 **to be written off sick** – *krankgeschrieben*
8 **I'm the happiest person alive** – *ich bin der glücklichste Mensch der Welt*

with me through the hallway[1]. "You can't imagine how happy I am."

I'm relatively surprised that my sister just assumes[2] that I've sorted[3] everything with Maik by myself[4]. After all, there's plenty that could have gone wrong[5]; and I say exactly that to her.

She looks at me, wide-eyed. "But I just arranged everything with Maik myself! He asked me if I wanted to go to the winter sports ball with him – and I said yes. And he thinks I'm great."

"You can't see into the future[6], can you?" For a second, I wonder if my sister actually has supernatural[7] capabilities. Or perhaps she's mad with fever and has no idea what she's saying.

"You don't need to be able to see into the future," she says, laughing as she throws her shoe into the corner, "he told me himself. Two hours ago, right where you're standing now."

This must be a case of serious fever. I've got to get her back to bed before she goes completely crazy[8]. Then I'll need to call mum. And then the doctor.

"We had a pizza and then we went for a walk, and he's just brought me back," continues my sister. "Why are you looking so funny

Love-Question 4
☑ INBOX
from: Mum Mobile

Hi Marie! R u feeling okay? How is ur sister? Hope u 2 got a lot of bedrest! Will b home later. xxx

· · · · · · · · ·

1 **hallway** – *Diele*
2 **to assume that/sth.** – *etw. annehmen, von etw. ausgehen*
3 **to sort** (Umgangssprache) – *regeln*
4 **by oneself** – *alleine*
5 **there's plenty that could have gone wrong** – *es hätte einiges schiefgehen können*
6 **to see into the future** – *hellsehen*
7 **supernatural** – *übersinnlich*
8 **to go crazy** – *rumspinnen*

at me[1]? Do you think I used too much eye-shadow? When he rang this morning I didn't have much time and I ..."

"Wait a second. Take it nice and slowly," I say and sit down on the floor.

Hanna bends down and looks at me, horrified. "What's the matter with you? What do you look like?[2] You didn't get in a fight[3] did you?"

"It was a snowball," I mumble, "now, I need you to be very clear and sensible for a sec[4], OK? Just for a teeny-weeny little[5] second. You say you've seen Maik – but I was on a sledge with him all day. Something is wrong there!"

Hanna sits down next to me on the floor, puts her arm around me and says: "Oh no. Oh no, no, no ... I think quite a lot has gone wrong!" Then she explains the situation to me[6]. Ann-Kathrin, Maik and Helena were supposed to get a lift from[7] Ann-Kathrin's father. As his car broke down, however, the three of them didn't make it on time[8]. "Helena got on the tram and went straight home because the bus had gone," she says. "And Ann-Kathrin and Maik rung me and asked if they could come and see me. Ann-Kathrin went after an hour or so, and Maik ..." She smiles dreamily[9]: "I'd never have thought it was as easy as that."

"How nice for you," I say after I've got over[10] the first shock. Suddenly, I feel very tired, "but do you think you can tell me who

· · · · · · · ·

1 **to look at sb. funny** – *jdm. komisch angucken*
2 **What do you look like?** – *Wie siehst du denn aus?*
3 **to get in a fight** – *in eine Schlägerei geraten*
4 **sec** (Umgangssprache) – *(Abkürzung für) Sekunde*
5 **teeny-weeny little** – *klitzeklein*
6 **to explain the situation to sb.** – *jdn. aufklären*
7 **to get a lift from sb. somewhere** – *von jdm. im Auto irgendwohin gebracht werden*
8 **to make it on time** – *es rechtzeitig schaffen*
9 **dreamily** – *verträumt*
10 **to get over sth.** – *über etw. hinwegkommen*

the other boy was? You know, the one who I thought was Maik. I spent a whole day flirting with him so that he'll come to the ball with you!" Hanna doesn't say anything for a while. Usually, she's got something to say for herself[1], but now …

"You know, I tried to call you," she says, "I wanted to tell you that Ann-Kathrin and Maik wouldn't be there and that you could relax. I didn't know that you were going to …"

"He was the only one left over and so I just assumed that he was Maik," I say. As I think of him, I warm up again, but now Hanna is looking at me.

"I think you've got a fever," she says and puts her hand on my forehead, "you're really hot. You should go straight to bed." Then her mobile phone rings and she's about to jump up to get it, but I hold her back. She's not getting out of it this easily[2]!

"I want to know who this boy was," I hiss, "because if you seriously think[3] that I've been out chatting up[4] some boy and getting my face messed up[5] just for you to send me to bed, you're wrong! I at least want to know who he was!" After I while, I add a description[6]: "He's got dark hair, dark eyes and is a bit bigger than me."

"Jonathan perhaps? Or Frederik? Or Lars?"

I just roll my eyes . What does she think I'm going to do? Suddenly say "stop! It was him!"? Then Hanna stands up. Perhaps she has realised that we're not making any progress as it is[7]. I hear her moving stuff in her room, swearing under her breath[8] and then

· · · · · · · · ·

1 **Usually, she's got something to say for herself …** – *Normalerweise fällt ihr immer etw. ein …*
2 **she's not getting out of it this easily** – *so einfach kommt sie mir nicht davon*
3 **If you seriously think …** – *Wenn du allen Ernstes glaubst …*
4 **to chat sb. up** (Umgangssprache) – *jdn. anbaggern*
5 **to mess up** – *ramponieren*
6 **description** – *Beschreibung*
7 **to make progress** – *weiterkommen*
8 **swearing under her breath** – *leise vor sich hin fluchend*

having a medium[1] coughing fit. An hour ago, I would have got up and gotten her a glass of water; but now I can't be bothered[2] and I'm feeling too tired.

"So, let's have a look," she says, coming back into the room with a pile[3] of photos, "these are photos from the beginning of high-school onwards. Just have a look through them …" She laughs, embarrassed: "I can't help you, because I don't know who you …"

"Stop right there![4]" I hold her still: "You're staying here so you can tell me who he is." Then I work my way through[5] the photos: at the school's country activity centre[6], days spent hiking[7], Christmas parties, class celebrations. Whoever it was who took these pictures, he has a real talent for bad photography. If Hanna weren't my twin[8] I wouldn't have recognised her in a single picture. "He's got dark hair, kind of medium length, and dark eyes," I repeat.

"That's just too imprecise," she says, shaking her head, "there are 15 boys in my class."

"And he's got a couple of spots on his chin!"

"They all have!" she says, laughing.

"OK, and he's kind of quiet, but very …" I search for the right word, "very … caring[9]." It sounds like an old-fashioned[10] word, but suddenly Hanna is very sure.

"That can only be Carl," she says and points at[11] one of the photos,

· · · · · · · · ·

1 **medium** – *mittlere*
2 **I can't be bothered** – *ich habe keine Lust*
3 **pile** – *Stapel*
4 **Stop right there!** (Redewendung) – *Halt! Stopp!*
5 **to work one's way through sth.** – *sich durch etw. arbeiten*
6 **country activity centre** – *Landheim*
7 **to hike** – *wandern*
8 **If Hanna weren't my twin …** – *Wenn Hanna nicht meine Zwillingsschwester wäre …*
9 **caring** – *fürsorglich*
10 **old-fashioned** – *altmodisch*
11 **to point at sth.** – *auf etw. deuten*

"him, here. What do you think?"

I squint[1]. It could just about[2] be the boy I mean. "I think so," I reply after a while.

"Well, that's all OK then," says Hanna. Why is she always so happy? "So now you know that you went sledging with Carl and that I've got Maik. Now, I've really got to give him a ring – the ball is on Saturday. Well, you know." She looks slightly uneasy as I shake my head. "OK, sorry, I know I forgot to say thanks to you[3], but if I do that now, will everything be alright?"

"No! Nothing will be alright!" I shout: "Carl thinks you're in love with him – can you imagine what'll happen[4] if you show up to the ball with Maik?"

"Oh, he'll get over that. It could be worse. Anyway ..." She looks at me mistrustfully[5]: "You guys didn't kiss, did you? Because that wasn't part of the deal[6], you know!"

"Of course we didn't kiss! Nevertheless, I think it's pretty unfair to just roll up[7] with Maik. Carl is such a nice guy and ..." Hanna looks at me while I talk.

"You've fallen in love with him!" she states[8] objectively[9].

I shake my head, try to say something pointless[10], but – damnit! – I can't. I just start crying.

"You OK?" says Hanna, holding a pack of tissues[11] under my nose

· · · · · · · · ·

1 **to squint** – *die Augen zusammenkneifen*
2 **It could just about ...** – *Es könnte vielleicht ....*
3 **to say thanks to sb.** – *sich bei jdm. bedanken*
4 **Can you imagine what'll happen ...** – *Was glaubst du, was los sein wird ...*
5 **mistrustfully** – *misstrauisch*
6 **... that wasn't part of the deal.** (Redewendung) – *... das war so nicht abgemacht.*
7 **to roll up** (Umgangssprache) – *antanzen*
8 **to state** – *feststellen*
9 **objectively** – *objektiv, neutral*
10 **pointless** – *belanglos*
11 **tissue** – *Papiertaschentuch*

that she has magically conjured up[1] out of her pocket. "Marie, there's no need to cry[2]," she says, putting her arm around me and smiling broadly[3], "after all, everything went very well actually, if you think about it. I've finally got Maik, and now you've got Carl. You'd make a lovely couple[4]. And we'll all go to the winter sports ball together – perfect!"

"But we can't. Carl thinks that I'm Hanna and has no idea that you have a twin!"

"If Carl really loves you, then he won't give a damn about whether you're called Hanna or Marie." Then she looks around for her mobile, which has started ringing again. Judging by the look in her eyes[5], it can only be Maik. She wants to answer, but I shake my head. We have other problems on our hands[6] at the moment, and we need to concentrate on them first. Hanna slumps[7] into the chair opposite me and looks pretty clueless[8].

"What do you want me to do?" she asks: "Go to Carl and say: 'Sorry, it's all a terrible mix-up[9] but luckily my twin sister has fallen in love with you. And look, we're identical twins[10], so it doesn't matter at all which one you get'?" I'm ill, by the way, and should probably go to bed." She finishes with a demonstrative[11] yawn[12].

I'm about to tell Hanna that I've had a pretty tiring day – and a swollen nose – when the doorbell rings.

· · · · · · · · ·

1 **to magically conjure up** – *(herbei)zaubern*
2 **there's no need to cry** – *du musst doch nicht heulen*
3 **broadly** – *breit*
4 **You'd make a lovely couple.** – *Ihr würdet ein hübsches Pärchen abgeben.*
5 **Judging by the look in her eyes ...** – *Ihrem Blick nach zu urteilen ...*
6 **on our hands** – *an der Backe, am Hals*
7 **to slump** – *zusammensacken*
8 **clueless** – *ratlos*
9 **mix-up** – *Verwechslung*
10 **identical twins** – *eineiige Zwillinge*
11 **demonstrative** – *demonstrativ*
12 **yawn** – *Gähnen*

"That's got to be Niederegger[1]!" whispers Hanna: "She's been annoying me all afternoon, telling me I should do her shopping and take Lohengrin for his walkies[2]."

"Let's just pretend that we're not here – or sleeping already!" I whisper back. The doorbell rings a couple more times, but we don't relent[3]. After all, it is already half past eight and we're just two seriously ill thirteen-year-olds who need their sleep.

"Well there you go," I say as the doorbell stops ringing, "I'm off to bed[4] and we can talk about the rest tomorrow. Somehow, I get the feeling that we need ..." I can't finish because the telephone rings and, in the blink of an eye[5], Hanna has picked up and breathed[6] "Hello" into the receiver[7]. A couple of seconds later, she passes me the phone and looks horrified:

"It's Carl!"

My heart is beating fast[8] when I hear his voice. Damnit! Why the hell did I let myself get dragged into[9] this silly little game? At that moment, however, I realise that this is no longer a game.

"I've still got a couple of things of yours in my rucksack," I hear him say, "I thought that you might need them, so I rang your doorbell but you didn't answer."

"Yeah, I was ... I think I was already asleep," I say. My voice sounds very quiet and Hanna looks at me pityingly. "Well, I didn't hear anything; you can give me the stuff another time."

. . . .

1 **That's got to be Niederegger!** – *Garantiert die Niederegger!*
2 **walkies** – *Gassi*
3 **to not relent** – *hart bleiben, nicht nachgeben*
4 **to be off to bed** – *schlafen gehen*
5 **in the blink of an eye** – *blitzschnell*
6 **to breath** – *hier: hauchen*
7 **recevier** – *Hörer*
8 **my heart is beating fast** – *mein Herz klopft*
9 **to let oneself get dragged into sth.** – *sich in etw. hineinziehen lassen*

"Hmm, I'd kind of like to get it done[1] this evening." I hear this and shut my eyes for a moment. Oh God, when he finds out that I'm not Hanna … And he'll find out for sure – it's not hard. It's such a shame, it could have all been so nice[2]. What I'd really like to do is to forget everything and start all over again[3] – but as Marie this time!

"Well, listen," I say, trying to hold back the tears[4], "I'm pretty tired after the day we've had and my face still hurts. Can't we talk about it another time? Or can you just leave the stuff in front of the door?"

"You've got to win some time," whispers Hanna and nods, satisfied, after I put Carl on speakerphone[5], "and we'll think of something." Carl is quiet for a moment. "Are you still there?" I ask, carefully.

"Of course," he says – he sounds tired too. Then, after a pause, he speaks again. "Maik thinks we should sort it out tonight."

"Maik?" says Hanna, tearing[6] the receiver out of my hand, "what's going on here? Is this supposed to be a joke or something[7]?"

Unfortunately, it's not a joke. I take the receiver back and say: "I just don't know any more." Carl bursts out laughing[8] at this, but he sounds pretty depressed[9].

"Maik lives in the building next to mine. We know each other pretty well and he just told me that he's going to the winter sports ball with you. So you can understand why we want an explana-

· · · · · · · · ·

1 **to get sth. done** – *etw. erledigen*
2 **it could have all been so nice** – *es hätte alles so schön sein können*
3 **to start all over again** – *von vorne anfangen*
4 **to hold back the tears** – *die Tränen zurückhalten*
5 **speakerphone** – *Lautsprecher*
6 **to tear** – *reißen*
7 **Is this supposed to be a joke or something?** (Redewendung) – *Soll das ein Witz sein, oder was?*
8 **to burst out laughing** – *auflachen*
9 **depressed** – *deprimiert*

tion[1], Hanna."

My sister and I look at each other and then nod, almost at the same time.

"OK, meet me in ten minutes time in front of our building," I say and hang up. Of course, it takes a little longer than ten minutes until we've agreed how we're going to do ourselves up. We put on woolly hats so that you can't see my long hair and it's almost half past nine by the time we open the door to our building as fully identical twins. You can only see that my nose is swollen if you really look closely[2].

"No!" shout Carl and Maik at the same time.

"Oh yes," we reply, "we're Marie and Hanna, identical twins, as you can see."

Carl only needs a second and points to me.

I smile at him. "Yeah, with that nose, it's not hard, is it?" I say.

"No," he says and looks at me so tenderly that I feel weak at the knees[3]. "But somehow I'd always recognise you. You are you, even though you look like your sister." He's about to say something else, but as he starts, Mrs Niederegger opens the shutters[4] in her living room and opens the window.

"What's all this racket[5] at night?" she shouts: "Poor Lohengrin can't sleep with this noise!"

"Well, let's talk about everything tomorrow," says Hanna, who is visibly[6] relieved[7] that everything has worked out so well[8], "because

• • • • • • • • •

1 **to want an explanation** – *eine Erklärung verlangen*
2 **to look closely** – *genau hinschauen*
3 **to feel weak at the knees** – *weiche Knie bekommen*
4 **shutters** – *Fensterladen, Rollladen*
5 **What's all this racket?** – *Was ist denn das für ein Lärm?*
6 **visibly** – *augenscheinlich, sichtbar*
7 **relieved** – *froh, erleichtert*
8 **to work out well** – *glimpflich ausgehen*

poor little Lohengrin really must have his sleep."
She gives Maik a kiss and then says that she would really love to
go for a late-night stroll[1].

"I think all this snow is very romantic," she adds as Maik hesi-
tates[2] and, before he can say anything, she's grabbed his hand and
they're off, leaving me with Carl in front of the door. He doesn't
say anything, he just looks at me. And I just look back. I can't tear
myself away[3] and it feels as if my heart is in my throat[4]. I can hear
Lohengrin barking in the background as I take a step towards Carl.
Then I just kiss him.

"Marie," I hear him say, "my Marie."
We stand there, hugging tightly[5]
and I'm so happy that I'd like to
dance with the snowflakes[6].

> Love-Question 5
> ☑ INBOX
> from: Hanna Mobile
>
> And? Did u kiss him?
> xxx

. . . .
1 **late-night stroll** – *Nachtspaziergang*
2 **to hesitate** – *zögern*
3 **to tear oneself away** – *sich losreißen*
4 **as if my heart is in my throat** – hier: *das Herz klopt mir bis zum Hals*
5 **hugging tightly** – *eng umschlungen*
6 **snowflake** – *Schneeflocke*

SMS-GLOSSAR

camera phone
Foto-Handy

inbox
Eingang

mobile (phone)
Handy

pay as you go
Prepaid

photo message
MMS

predictive text
Texterkennung

text sb.
jdn. ansimsen

text message
SMS

4 — for
für

2 — to; too
zu, auf; auch

2gether — together
zusammen

l8 — late
spät

w8 — wait
warten

b — be
sein

c — see
sehen

r — are
bist, seid

u — you
du, euer

ur — your; you're
dein, euer; du bist,
ihr seid

hun — honey
Schatz

gonna — going to
werden

alrite — alright/OK
OK, in Ordnung

kinda — kind of
irgendwie

wanna — want to
möchten

lol - laughing out
loud
laut lachend

cul8r - see you later
bis später

b/f - boyfriend
Freund

bday - birthday
Geburtstag

x - kiss
Kuss

NÜTZLICHE AUSDRÜCKE ZUM THEMA LIEBE

ask sb. out	jdn. zu einem Date einladen
be crazy / mad about sb.	in jdn. verknallt sein
be heartbroken	todunglücklich sein
be lovesick	Liebeskummer haben
chat sb. up	jdn. anmachen
chat-up line	Anmachspruch
cheat on sb.	jdn. betrügen
couple	Pärchen
dump sb.	mit jdm. Schluss machen
fall in love with sb.	sich in jdn. verlieben
have butterflies in one's stomach	Schmetterlinge im Bauch haben
hug	sich umarmen
in a relationship	vergeben
kiss	küssen
loveletter	Liebesbrief
single	Single; solo
secret note	Geheimbotschaft
shy	schüchtern
snog	knutschen

WORTLISTE

A

a face I know	*ein bekanntes Gesicht*
a few minutes later	*kurze Zeit später*
a foot or so	*ungefähr ein halber Meter*
a good way	*ein gutes Stück*
a nice way of telling you about it	*eine schonende Art, dir das beizubringen*
a pile of	hier: *jede Menge*
accept one's fate	*sich seinem Schicksal fügen*
actually	*in Wirklichkeit*
admit	*zugeben*
advise sb. against sth.	*jdm. von etw. abraten*
ajar	*angelehnt*
all the while	*die ganze Zeit*
almost touched	*fast gerührt*
altogether	*gänzlich, vollständig*
and besides	*außerdem*
and stuff (Umgangssprache)	*und so*
and we have to put a stop to that with every means at our disposal	*und das gilt es mit allen Mitteln zu verhindern*
answer	hier: *rangehen*
answering machine	*Anrufbeantworter*
anytime today'll do (Redewendung)	*wenn's geht, heute noch*
apart from that	*außerdem*
approvingly	*anerkennend*
Are you kidding me?	*Willst du mich reinlegen?*
Are you nuts?	*Spinnst du?*
argue	hier: *herumdiskutieren*
artificial	*künstlich*
as a deputy	*vertretungsweise*
as far as I'm concerned	*für mich*
as if he can't believe his luck	*als ob er sein Glück nicht fassen kann*
as if he was trying to make it onto the silver screen	hier: *kinoreif*
as if my heart is in my throat	hier: *das Herz klopt mir bis zum Hals*
as it happens	*in der Tat, tatsächlich*
as it is	*auch so schon*

Right at top of first entry: hier: *(die Schulnote) Eins*

aspiring	*aufstrebend*
assign	*zuteilen*
as stupid as I am (Redewendung)	*ich blöde Kuh*
assume that/sth.	*etw. annehmen, von etw. ausgehen*
astonished	*erstaunt*
at this of all times	*ausgerechnet jetzt*
at your place (Umgangssprache)	*bei dir zu Hause*
attempt	*Versuch*
average	*durchschnittlich, nichtssagend*
awestruck	*ehrfürchtig*
awkward	*unbehaglich*
awkward situation	*blöde Situation*
back out	*abspringen*
bag sth. (Umgangssprache)	*sich etw. unter den Nagel reißen*
barefoot	*barfuß*
bark at sb.	*jdn. anbellen*
be about to do sth.	*kurz davor sein, etw. zu tun*
be chatting away	*quatschen*
be concerned with sth.	*Rücksicht auf etw. nehmen*
be crazy about sb./so.	*für jdn./etw. schwärmen*
be flabbergasted	*aus allen Wolken fallen*
be into sb. (Umgangssprache)	*auf jdn. stehen*
be into sth. (Umgangssprache)	*auf etw. stehen*
be left with nobody	*das Nachsehen haben*
be off (Umgangssprache)	*weg sein*
be off to bed	*schlafen gehen*
be on at sb. to do sth.	*jdm. damit in den Ohren liegen, etw. zu tun*
be on the phone to sb.	*mit jdm. am Telefon sprechen*
be pretty hard work	*ganz schön anstrengend sein*
be satisfied with sth.	*mit etw. zufrieden sein*
be stressed out	*im Stress sein*
be up for sth.	*auf etw. Lust haben*
be written off sick	*krankgeschrieben*
beam at sb.	*jdn. anstrahlen*
beaten down (Umgangssprache)	*geschafft*
beep	*piepsen*
before you know it	*im Handumdrehen, ruck, zuck*
beforehand	*vorher*

behind the counter	*hinter der Theke*
behind the curtains	*hinter der Gardine*
bend	*Kurve*
bet	*wetten*
bladder	*Blase*
blank	hier: *verständnislos*
bleed	*bluten*
blurt out	*herausplatzen*
board	hier: *Anzeigetafel*
bootlaces	*Schnürsenkel*
brave	*mutig, stark*
break down	*eine Panne haben*
break down in tears	*in Tränen ausbrechen*
breath	hier: *hauchen*
bright red	*knallrot*
bring sb. back down to earth	*jdn. auf den Boden der Tatsachen zurück-holen*
broadly	*breit*
brusque	*knapp, schroff*
bunk off school	*blaumachen, Schule schwänzen*
burst out laughing	*auflachen*
business	hier: *Angelegenheit*
but just sitting around won't make it happen!	*allein vom Rumsitzen wird das bestimmt nichts!*
by force	*mit Gewalt*
by oneself	*alleine*
by this stage	*zu diesem Zeitpunkt*
by way of closing	*abschließend, schließlich*
by way of making it up to him	*als Wiedergutmachung*
calm down	*sich beruhigen*
Can you imagine what'll happen ...	*Was glaubst du, was los sein wird ...*
careful	*vorsichtig*
caring	*fürsorglich*
casual	*beiläufig*
catch sth.	*sich anstecken, sich etw. einfangen*
catty	*zickig*
cause trouble	*Stress machen*
chat sb. up (Umgangssprache)	*jdn. anbaggern*
cheat	*Betrüger*

cheating	*Schummeln, Mogeln*
chestnut tree	*Kastanienbaum*
chew one's bottom lip	*auf seiner Unterlippe herumkauen*
chomp through (Umgangssprache)	hier: *verdrücken*
chubby	*pummelig*
chuck (Umgangssprache)	*werfen, schmeißen*
circuit training	*Zirkeltraining*
claim	*behaupten*
classmates	*Klassenkamaraden*
club	hier: *Schläger*
clueless	*ratlos*
cock one's ears	*die Ohren spitzen*
come undone	*aufgehen*
come up to sb.	*auf jdn. zukommen*
comfort sb.	*jdn. trösten*
comfortingly	*beruhigend*
complete madness	*völliger geistiger Verwirrung*
concerned	*besorgt*
conclude	*schlussfolgern*
confess one's love to sb.	*jdm. seine Liebe gestehen*
confident	*selbstbewusst*
confused	*irritiert*
congratulations	*Glückwunsch, Gratulation*
conserve energy	hier: *Energie aufbewahren*
considering the fact that	*dafür, dass*
contradict sb.	*jdm. widersprechen*
cool about this kind of stuff	hier: *so locker*
coolly	*lässig*
corny	*kitschig*
herbal-cough tea	*Hustentee*
coughing fit	*Hustenanfall*
count on sb.	*auf jdn. zählen*
country activity centre	*Landheim*
cross one's arms over one's chest	*die Arme vor der Brust verschränken*
cross one's fingers	*die Daumen drücken*
crossing	hier: *Kreuzung*
curious	*neugierig*
curt	*knapp, schroff*
dab	*tupfen*

dachshund	*Dackel, Dachshund*
Dammit! (Umgangssprache)	*Verflixt!*
dash off	*losrennen*
deaf	*taub*
deal with sth./sb.	*es mit jdm./etw. aufnehmen*
decide sth.	hier: *den Ausschlag geben*
decisively	*entschieden*
declarations of true love	*Liebesschwüre*
demonstrative	*demonstrativ*
depressed	*deprimiert*
description	*Beschreibung*
desperately	*krampfhaft*
detour	*Abstecher*
devastation	*Verwüstung*
disappear	*verschwinden*
disbelieving	*ungläubig*
disinterested	*desinteressiert*
do sb. good	*jdm. guttun*
do sb. up (Umgangssprache)	*jdn. aufmotzen, aufbrezeln*
done for (Umgangssprache)	*gelaufen, im Eimer*
done up (Umgangssprache)	*aufgebrezelt*
drag oneself	*sich schleppen*
drama club	*Theaterclub*
draw	hier: *auslosen*
draw first prize	*das große Los ziehen*
dreamily	*verträumt*
dried	*getrocknet*
drop out	*ausfallen*
dull pain	*schmerzlindernd wirken*
elbow someone gently	*jdn. leicht anstoßen*
embarrassedly	*verlegen*
emotionally	*gerührt, emotional*
emphasise	*betonen, unterstreichen*
emphatically	*betont*
encouragingly	*aufmunternd*
especially	*extra*
etc	hier: *und so*
evening rush-hour	*Feierabendverkehr*
excuse	*Ausrede*

explain the situation to sb.	jdn. aufklären
expressly	ausdrücklich
extremely careful	äußerst vorsichtig
eyeliner	Lidstrich
fake	unecht
fall head-over-heels in love	sich heftigst verlieben
fall ill	krank werden
falter	stolpern
familiarisation	Gewöhnung
fascinated	fasziniert
fate	Schicksal
fatty (Umgangssprache)	Dickerchen, Pummelchen
feebly	lahm, schwach
feel weak at the knees	weiche Knie bekommen
fiddle around with sth.	mit etw. herumfummeln
figure sth. out (Umgangssprache)	etw. kapieren
find out	rausbekommen
fir tree	Tannenbaum
first-hand	aus erster Hand
fit as a fiddle	total fit, kerngesund
fluffy	Plüsch-
fog	Nebel
football or not!	Fußball hin oder her!
for a bit	für paar Minuten, ein Stündchen
for once	ausnahmsweise
for safekeeping	hier: um sie aufzubewahren
forehead	Stirn
forgiveness	Verzeihung
freeze to death	erfrieren
friendship-bracelet	Freundschaftsbändchen
from year nine	aus der neunten Klasse
frown	die Stirn runzeln
gaggle	Schar
gangway	Mittelgang
gasp	röcheln
gather up all one's courage	seinen ganzen Mut zusammennehmen
gently	hier: vorsichtig
get	hier: treffen, erwischen
get a craving for sth.	Heißhunger auf etw. bekommen

get a grip of oneself	sich wieder fassen
get a lift from sb. somewhere	von jdm. im Auto irgendwohin gebracht werden
get a move on (Umgangssprache)	sich ranhalten
get annoyed	sauer werden, sich aufregen
get cold	frieren
get free of sth.	sich von etw. befreien
get hold of someone (Umgangssprache)	jdn. (telefonisch) erwischen
get in a fight	in eine Schlägerei geraten
get in real trouble	gewaltigen Ärger kriegen
get it	hier: kapieren
get over sb./sth.	über jdn./etw. hinwegkommen
get practice	Übung bekommen
get roped into doing sth. (Umgangssprache)	gezwungen werden, etw. zu tun
get sb. bad	jdn. richtig erwischen
get sth. done	etw. erledigen
get stuck in one's throat	im Hals stecken bleiben
get the feeling that ...	den Eindruck bekommen, dass ...
giggle	kichern
give away	hier: verraten
give sb. goose bumps	bei jdm. eine Gänsehaut verursachen
give sb. space	jdm. Freiraum geben
give sth. a lot of thought	lange über etw. nachdenken
glow	glühen
glowing red	glutrot
go crazy	rumspinnen
go down	hier: abschwellen
go for (Umgangssprache)	hier: sich aussuchen
go on about sth.	von etw. schwafeln
go over things in one's mind	sich mit seinen Gedanken beschäftigen
go running into sb.'s arms	bei jdm. Trost suchen
go way overboard (Umgangssprache)	total übertreiben
go weak at the knees	weiche Knie bekommen
God no!	Bloß nicht!
Good one! (Umgangsprache)	Selten so gelacht!
gorgeous	traumhaft
Got that? (Umgangssprache)	Haste gehört?

grab sb.'s arm	*jdn. am Arm packen*
grateful	*dankbar*
guinea pig	hier: *Versuchskaninchen*
gulp down	*verschlingen*
gut feeling	*Bauchgefühl*
half-way	*halbwegs, einigermaßen*
hallway	*Diele*
handful	*eine Handvoll*
handmirror	*Kosmetikspiegel*
Hang on a sec! (Redewendung)	*Stopp mal! Halt!*
hang onto sb.	*sich an jdm. festklammern*
hang up	*aufhängen*
Hanna should count herself lucky she's got me as a sister.	*Hanna kann von Glück reden, dass ich ihre Schwester bin.*
hardly	*kaum*
Has he lost it completely? (Redewendung)	*Was glaubt er eigentlich?*
have a bit of a snog (Umgangssprache)	*rumknutschen*
have a go at sb.	*jdn. anschnauzen, anfahren*
have a knack for doing sth.	*ein Talent dafür haben, etw. zu tun*
have no choice other than to ...	*keine andere Wahl haben, außer zu ...*
have on	*tragen (Kleidung)*
have one's way	*sich durchsetzen*
hayfever	*Heuschnupfen*
He really should be making more a show.	hier: *Er hätte schon ein bisschen mehr Anteilnahme zeigen können.*
He'd be better off forgetting everything	*er wäre besser dran, alles zu vergessen*
He's a cutie	*er ist ein Süßer*
He's just asking for it! (Redewendung)	*Das schreit nach Rache!*
head tilted to the side	*mit schrägem Kopf*
head towards sb.	*auf jdn. zusteuern*
heartless	*herzlos*
hesitate	*zögern*
hike	*wandern*
hiss	*zischen, fauchen*
hit form	*zur Höchstform anlaufen*
hit on sth.	*auf etw. kommen*
hold back the tears	*die Tränen zurückhalten*
horde	*Horde*

horrifically	*grauenhaft*
horrified	*entsetzt*
hot off the press	*brühwarm*
how badly it hurts	*wie weh das tut*
hug	*umarmen, um den Hals fallen*
huge amounts	*Unmengen*
hugging tightly	*eng umschlungen*
hum	*summen*
I am a ticking time bomb of rage.	*Ich könnte jeden Moment vor Wut platzen.*
I can't be bothered	*ich habe keine Lust*
I can't be in two places at once (Redewendung)	*Ich kann mich nicht zerteilen*
I can't stand the idea of any more snow.	*Ich kann keinen Schnee mehr sehen.*
I don't buy that! (Umgangssprache)	*Das kaufe ich dir nicht ab!*
I hadn't imagined it like this.	*So hatte ich mir das nicht vorgestellt.*
I might just as well go home now.	*Ich könnte jetzt auch genauso gut nach Hause gehen.*
I really couldn't care less about Leo.	*Leo ist mir so was von egal.*
I really shouldn't have said it.	*Das hätte ich mir besser verkniffen.*
I take care of my appearance.	*Ich mache was aus meinem Typ.*
I think his chin is about to hit the floor.	*Ich habe den Eindruck, dass ihm gleich die Kinnlade runterfällt.*
I'll think of sth.	*Ich lasse mir etw. einfallen.*
I'm just not that up for it. (Umgangssprache)	*Ich habe irgendwie gar keine richtige Lust.*
I'm not going to let myself get treated like that! (Redewendung)	*Mit mir nicht!*
I'm not in the least intending to ...	*Ich habe nicht die geringste Absicht ...*
I'm off now (Umgangssprache)	*Ich bin dann mal weg*
I'm the happiest person alive	*Ich bin der glücklichste Mensch der Welt.*
I've had enough.	*Mir reicht es.*
I've had it up to here with you! (Redewendung)	*Ich bin so was von fertig mit dir!, Ich hab' die Schnauze voll von dir!*
identical twins	*eineiige Zwillinge*
If Hanna weren't my twin ...	*Wenn Hanna nicht meine Zwillingsschwester wäre ...*
If I'm at all lucky ...	*Mit ein wenig Glück ...*
If only Hanna knew!	*Wenn Hanna nur wüsste!*
If that's what they want to do.	*Wenn ihnen danach zumute ist.*

If you seriously think ...	*Wenn du allen Ernstes glaubst ...*
immature	*unreif*
impossible to misinterpret	*absolut eindeutig*
impractical	*unpraktisch*
in any case	*jedenfalls*
in case of emergency	*im Notfall*
in no time at all	*ruck, zuck*
in quite a hurry	*in ziemlicher Eile*
in the blink of an eye	*blitzschnell*
in the cold light of day	*bei Tageslicht betrachtet*
in the meantime	*in der Zwischenzeit*
in vain	*vergeblich*
incapable of doing sth.	*außerstande, etw. zu tun*
inconspicuously	*unauffällig*
indecisively	*unschlüssig*
independently	*unabhängig*
indignantly	*unwillig, entrüstet*
infer	*schlussfolgern*
inner voice	*innere Stimme*
inquisitively	*fragend*
insulted	*beleidigt*
interrupt	*unterbrechen*
irresistable	*unwiderstehlich*
Is this supposed to be a joke or something? (Redewendung)	*Soll das ein Witz sein, oder was?*
It could have all been so nice.	*Es hätte alles so schön sein können.*
It could just about ...	*Es könnte vielleicht ....*
It could well be that ... (Redewendung)	*Es kann durchaus sein, dass ...*
It dawns on me.	*Es dämmert mir.*
It rings for ages.	*Es klingelt ewig.*
It was well worth it.	*Es war es wert.*
It would appear that my mum is ...	*augenscheinlich ist meine Mutter ...*
It's a pack of lies.	hier: *alles Lügen*
It's all for a good cause. (Redewendung)	*Es dient schließlich einem guten Zweck.*
It's as if it's meant to be. (Redewendung)	*Es ist wie vorherbestimmt*
It's enough to make you cry. (Umgangsprache)	*Es ist zum Heulen.*
It's like when there's been a storm.	*Es ist wie nach einem Gewitter.*

It's not convenient.	*Es passt gerade nicht.*
item	hier: *Artikel*
jealously	*neidisch*
Judging by the look in her eyes ...	*Ihrem Blick nach zu urteilen ...*
jump	hier: *zusammenfahren*
jump the queue	*sich vordrängeln*
jump up	*aufspringen, losspurten*
just give me a shout (Umgangssprache)	*meld' dich einfach*
just in case	*vorsichtshalber*
just like that (Umgangssprache)	*ruck, zuck*
just now	*vorhin*
just show up	*einfach vorbeischauen*
just thinking about the fact that ...	*Schon allein bei der Vorstellung, dass ...*
just won't do (Redewendung)	*geht gar nicht*
keep eye-contact	*Augenkontakt halten*
keep on at it (Umgangssprache)	*so weitermachen*
keep the books	*Buchhaltung machen*
kiss on the cheek	*Kuss auf die Wange*
knackered (Umgangssprache)	*am Ende, fix und fertig*
kneel down	*sich herunterbeugen*
knit one's brown	*die Stirn runzeln*
lad (Umgangssprache)	*Junge, Typ*
lamentations	*Gejammer*
landlady	*Vermieterin*
last	hier: *aushalten, durchhalten*
late-night stroll	*Nachtspaziergang*
laugh oneself silly (Redewendung)	*sich krank lachen*
laugh out loud	*laut lachen*
laughing away	*lachend*
lean back	*sich zurücklehnen*
lean one's head back	*den Kopf nach hinten zu legen*
Leo will probably think I've gone completely crazy.	*Leo wird mich dann wohl für völlig durchgeknallt halten.*
let go	*loslassen*
Let her think out a way to ...	*Soll sie doch sehen, wie sie ...*
let one's mind wander	*seinen Gedanken freien Lauf lassen*
let oneself get dragged into sth.	*sich in etw. hineinziehen lassen*
let sth. count	*etw. gelten lassen*
like a bolt	*blitzschnell*

like a good little boy/girl	(ironisch) schön brav
like mad	wie verrückt, wie ein/e Irre/r
like there's anything I could do about it	als ob ich irgendwas dafür könnte
look at sb. funny	jdm. schief angucken
look closely	genau hinschauen
look like one has been in the wars (Redewendung)	einen ganz mitgenommenen Eindruck machen
look of surprise	Ausdruck der Überraschung
look out for number one (Redewendung)	sich auf seine eigenen Interessen konzentrieren.
look sb. up and down	jdn. von oben bis unten mustern
madly in love	total verknallt
magically conjure up	(herbei)zaubern
main entrance	Haupteingang
make a real scene	ein Riesentheater machen
make it on time	es rechtzeitig schaffen
make one's way	sich seinen Weg bahnen
make one's way through the crowd	sich einen Weg durch die Menge bahnen
make oneself sandwiches	sich Brote schmieren
make progress	weiterkommen
make sure	hier: sich überzeugen
make the first move	den ersten Schritt machen
making out	Knutscherei
manage to do sth.	es schaffen, etw. zu tun
matching	hier: passend
medium	mittlere
melt	schmelzen, dahinschmelzen
mess up	ramponieren
messed up (Umgangssprache)	bescheuert
miss one's calling	seine Berufung verfehlen
missing	fehlend
mistrustfully	misstrauisch
misunderstanding	Missverständnis
mittens	Fäustlinge
mix-up	Verwechslung
monotone	monoton, tonlos
move a bit closer to sb.	an jdn. heranrücken
mow the lawn	den Rasen mähen
mumble	nuscheln, murmeln

murmur	*murmeln*
muster	*aufbringen*
my heart is beating fast	*ich habe Herzklopfen*
my heart sinks	*mein Herz wird schwer*
nice and carefully	*schön vorsichtig*
no trace of ...	*keine Spur von ...*
nod	*nicken*
nonetheless	*immerhin*
not at all	*nicht im Geringsten*
not bat an eyelid	*nicht mit der Wimper zucken*
not be able to stand the sight of sth.	*etw. nicht sehen können*
not dare to do sth.	*sich etw. nicht trauen*
not fair-play	*nicht fair*
not have the foggiest (Umgangssprache)	*keinen blassen Schimmer haben*
not move a muscle (Redewendung)	*sich auch nur im Geringsten bewegen*
not quite catch sth.	*etw. nicht so genau verstehen*
not really notice sb.	*jdn. nicht so richtig wahrnehmen*
not relent	*hart bleiben, nicht nachgeben*
not to even think about doing sth. (Redewendung)	*nicht einmal daran denken, etw. zu tun*
noticeable	*spürbar*
nudge sb.	*jdn. anschubsen*
nursing	*Tätigkeit als Krankenschwester*
objectively	*objektiv, neutral*
occupy	*besetzen*
Off you go!	*Und los!*
offended	*beleidigt*
Oh come on!	*Ach komm schon!*
old-fashioned	*altmodisch*
on business	*für die Firma, dienstlich*
on our hands	*an der Backe, am Hals*
on the cheek	*auf die Wange*
on the double (Umgangssprache)	*schleunigst, umgehend*
on the look-out for	*auf der Suche nach*
once and for all	*ein für alle Mal*
One hell of a show! (Redewendung)	hier: *Superleistung!*
only have eyes for sb.	*nur Augen für jdn. haben*
onwards!	*vorwärts!*

opposite direction	Gegenrichtung
ordinary	alltäglich, banal
otherwise	sonst
our eyes cross	unsere Blicke treffen sich
out of breath	außer Atem
outraged	empört
overdressed	aufgedonnert
overtake	überholen
overwhelming enthusiasm	überwältigende Begeisterung
paddling pool	Planschbecken
painkiller	Schmerztablette
pale	blass
pant	hervorstoßen
pathetic	erbärmlich, lächerlich
peace and quiet (Redewendung)	Ruhe
pedal	in die Pedale treten
performance	Aufführung
person who's sent it	Absender
piglet	Schweinchen
pile	Stapel
pimple	Pickel(chen)
pinch	kneifen
play it by ear (Redewendung)	flexibel bleiben, improvisieren
play one's part to perfection	seine Rolle perfekt spielen
play the saviour	den Retter vorspielen, einen auf Tröster machen
playground	Pausenhof
plot of land	Grundstück
point at sth.	auf etw. deuten
pointless	belanglos
pot	Teekanne
pretend	so tun, also ob
pretend that	so tun als ob
pretty busy (Umgangssprache)	schön beschäftigt
psychologising	psychologisieren
pull	ziehen
pull a face	das Gesicht verziehen
pull oneself together	sich fassen, sich zusammenreißen
punch sb.	jdm. eine runterhauen

puppy-dog eyes (Redewendung)	*Hundeblick*
put away	*verstauen*
put on	hier: *aufsetzen*
put one's arm through sb.'s	*sich bei jdm. ein-/unterhaken*
put up one's hair	*seine Haare hochstecken*
put water on	*Wasser aufsetzen*
quieten things down	*für Ruhe zu sorgen*
rack	hier: *Gepäckträger*
rational	*nüchtern*
really notice	*bewusst wahrnehmen*
rearrange	*zurechtrücken*
reassuringly	*beruhigend*
recevier	*Hörer*
reckon (Umgangssprache)	*vermuten, denken*
refuse	*sich weigern*
refusing to believe	*ungläubig*
regress	hier: *zurückentwickeln*
relieved	*erleichtert, froh*
remaining strength	*letzte Kraft*
remains	*Reste*
remark	*feststellen*
resistance is futile (Redewendung)	*Widerstand ist zwecklos*
revealing	*den Blick freigebend auf*
right royal (Umgangssprache)	*... der sich gewaschen hat*
risk	*riskieren*
roll one's eyes	*die Augen verdrehen*
roll over	*sich auf die andere Seite drehen*
roll up (Umgangssprache)	*antanzen*
ruin	*verderben*
run a fever	*Fieber haben*
run across sb.	*jdm. über den Weg laufen*
run into sb.	*jdn. zufällig treffen*
rush into somewhere	*irgendwo hineinstürzen*
satisfied	*zufrieden*
say by way of advice	*raten*
say thanks to sb.	*sich bei jdm. bedanken*
cheesy song	*kitschiges Lied*
score	hier: *Tore schießen*
score (Umgangssprache)	hier: *jdn. klarmachen*

sec	(Abkürzung für) Sekunde
see into the future	hellsehen
Serves him right!	Geschieht ihm recht!
set off	losfahren
shake one's head	den Kopf schütteln
Shall we?	Wollen wir?
shamelessly	hier: hemmungslos
share	teilen
shatter	zerschlagen, zertrümmern
She hasn't even noticed I'm here.	Sie hat mich nicht mal wahrgenommen.
she's bound to ...	Sie wird bestimmt ...
She's not getting out of it this easily.	So einfach kommt sie mir nicht davon.
shout at sb.	jdn. anbrüllen
shove sth. at sb. (Umgangssprache)	jdm. etw. in die Hand drücken
show one's face	auftauchen, sich blicken lassen
show one's true colours	Farbe bekennen
show up (Umgangssprache)	aufkreuzen
shrill	schrill, gellend
shutters	Fensterladen, Rolladen
sigh	seufzen
sign sb. up	jdn. anmelden
sixth sense	sechster Sinn
size sb. up	jdn. mustern
slam	knallen, werfen
sledge	Schlitten fahren
sledging	Rodeln, Schlittenfahren
sleep in	ausschlafen
slightly odd taste	etwas merkwürdiger Geschmack
slink off	kleinlaut abziehen
slip out	rausrutschen
slump	zusammensacken
Smash!	Rums!
snog	knutschen
snowflake	Schneeflocke
sob	schluchzen
some kind of ...	so eine Art ...
something's not right here (Redewendung)	irgendetwas stimmt hier nicht!
sort (Umgangssprache)	regeln

sound	*ertönen*
speakerphone	*Lautsprecher*
speed up	*sich beeilen, Gas geben*
squint	*die Augen zusammenkneifen*
squirm on one's seat	*auf seinem Sitz herumrutschen*
stairwell	*Treppenhaus*
start afresh	*neu anfangen*
start all over again	*von vorne anfangen*
start an avalanche	*eine Lawine lostreten*
state	*feststellen*
stationers	*Schreibwarengeschäft*
stick one's tongue down someone's throat (Umgangssprache)	*jdm. die Zunge in den Hals stecken*
stop by at sb.'s	*bei jdm. vorbeischauen*
stop by somewhere	*irgendwo vorbeischauen*
stop oneself saying sth.	*sich etw. verkneifen*
Stop right there! (Redewendung)	*Halt! Stopp!*
Stop this rubbish!	*Hör auf damit!*
strap	*Schnur*
stress	hier: *betonen*
strewn	*verstreut*
strict	*streng*
strike while the iron is hot	*das Eisen schmieden, solange es heiß ist*
stroke	*streicheln, kraulen*
struggle through sth.	*sich durch etw. quälen*
stuck to each other	*aneinander geklebt*
stylish	*chic, modisch*
suddenly	*plötzlich, schlagartig*
suit each other	*zusammenpassen*
suit sb. well	*jdm. gelegen kommen*
sunbathing	*Sonnenbaden*
supernatural	*übersinnlich*
suspect	*mutmaßen*
swan out	*majestätisch herausschweben*
swear true love	*wahre Liebe schwören*
swearing under her breath	*leise vor sich hin fluchend*
swell up	*zuschwellen*
Swiss chard	*Mangold*
tack on (Umgangssprache)	*hinzufügen*

take a deep breath	*tief durchatmen*
take care of sth. onesself	*etw. selbst erledigen*
take one's pick	*sich etw. aussuchen*
tap	*tippen*
tear	*reißen*
tear oneself away	*sich losreißen*
teeny-weeny little	*klitzeklein*
test sb.'s fitness to the limit	*jdm. alles abverlangen*
text	hier: *SMS*
Thank God	*Gott sei Dank*
That mean's you too.	*Das gilt auch für dich.*
That really is more than enough.	*Das reicht jetzt wirklich.*
That sounds all well and good, but … (Redewendung)	*Das klingt zwar alles schön und gut, aber …*
That was a close one (Redewendung)	*Das war knapp!*
That wasn't part of the deal. (Redewendung)	*Das war so nicht abgemacht.*
That's certainly the impression I get. (Redewendung)	*So scheint es jedenfalls.*
That's got to be Niederegger!	*Garantiert die Niederegger!*
That's just too bad! (Redewendung)	*Pech geabt!*
That's just what he deserves (Redewendung)	*Das hat er verdient!*
That's not a real lie.	*Das ist nicht mal richtig geschwindelt.*
the best bit	*das Allerbeste*
the best idea ever (Umgangssprache)	*eine Wahnsinnsidee*
the chances	*die Wahrscheinlichkeit*
the lesser of two evils	*das kleinere Übel*
The only point on which I don't compromise.	*Der einzige Punkt, bei dem ich hart bleibe.*
the other class in our year	*Parallelklasse*
the whole kit and caboodle (Umgangssprache)	*alles Drum und Dran*
There was nothing going on with Vanessa.	*Mit Vanessa lief nichts.*
There's no need to cry.	*Du musst doch nicht heulen.*
There's plenty that could have gone wrong.	*Es hätte einiges schiefgehen können.*
think hard	*schwer überlegen*

think to oneself	*sich denken*
This also gives me the chance to ...	*Bei der Gelegenheit kann ich auch ...*
This really is the last thing I need. (Redewendung)	*Das hat mir gerade noch gefehlt.*
threat	*Drohung*
tidy up	*wieder in Ordnung bringen*
tidy up one's room	*sein Zimmer aufräumen*
tissue	*Papiertaschentuch*
toboggan	*rodeln, Schlitten fahren*
toboggan run	*Rodelbahn*
touched	*gerührt*
traffic light	*Ampel*
trajectory	*Flugbahn*
tremble	*zittern*
turn up (Umgangssprache)	*antanzen, aufkreuzen*
turtle-neck jumper	*Rollkragenpullover*
unbearable	*unerträglich, unmöglich*
unbelievably	*unglaublich*
under one's breath	*halblaut*
uneasily	*unsicher*
uneasy	*flau, unsicher*
unfortunate	*unvorteilhaft*
unpleasant	*unangenehm*
uphill	*bergaufwärts*
urge	*Bedürfnis*
Usually, she's got something to say for herself ...	*Normalerweise fällt ihr immer etw. ein ...*
utter	*von sich geben*
utterly	*ganz, völlig*
vague	*vag*
vanish	*verschwinden*
visibly	*augenscheinlich, sichtbar*
vocabulary	*Wortschatz*
voicemail	*Mailbox*
volume	*Lautstärke*
walk up to sb.	*jdm. entgegenkommen*
walkies	*Gassi*
want an explanation	*eine Erklärung verlangen*
warm up	*hier: sich einspielen*

wave over to sb.	*jdm. zuwinken*
wave sth. about	*mit etw. herumfuchteln*
We had agreed that ...	*Wir hatten ausgemacht, dass ...*
We'll be fine	*Das haben wir gleich*
We're just closing!	*Wir schließen gerade!*
We've been wanting to ...	*Wir wollten ...*
weary	*matt, schwach, flau*
weigh	hier: *abwiegen*
What do you look like?	*Wie siehst du denn aus?*
What does Niederegger think she's doing ...?	*Was fällt Niederegger bloß ein ...?*
What does that look like! (Redewendung)	*Wie sieht das denn aus!*
What girls have always known how to do.	hier: *Was Mädchen schon immer beherr-schen.*
what the matter is (Redewendung)	*was ist los ist.*
what with me living just a couple of streets down the road	*da ich ja nur paar Straßen weiter wohne*
What's all this racket?	*Was ist denn das für ein Lärm?*
What's going on here?	*Was ist denn hier los?*
which isn't a lie	*was nicht gelogen ist*
while all this was happening	*inzwischen*
while you're at it (Umgangssprache)	*wo du schon dabei bist*
whinging	*quengelnd*
whisper	*flüstern*
whistle	hier: *Schiedsrichterpfeife*
win someone's heart	*jdns. Herz im Sturm erobern*
wiry-haired	*Rauhhaar-*
with a margin	*mit Rand*
with a sigh	*seufzend*
with an air of mystery	*geheimnisvoll*
with that	*darauf hin*
withheld	*unterdrückt*
without a shred of pity	*ohne eine Spur von Mitleid*
without even trying	*locker, mit links*
without paying any attention to sth.	*ohne auf etw. zu achten*
work it out by oneself (Umgangssprache)	*selber drauf kommen*
work one's way through sth.	*sich durch etw. arbeiten*
work out	hier: *kapieren*
work out well	*glimpflich ausgehen*

working on	*auf Basis von*
worried	*besorgt, bekümmert*
Would you mind?	*Bist du so lieb?*
wrap	*wickeln*
writhe	*sich winden*
yawn	*Gähnen*
Yeah, right!	*Von wegen!*
yell	*brüllen*
You bet! (Umgangssprache)	*Exakt!, Aber klar!*
You can go ahead and ...	*Du kannst ruhig ...*
You can't miss it.	*Das kannst du dir nicht entgehen lassen.*
You don't mind, do you?	*Du hast nichts dagegen, oder?*
You have to see it to believe it. (Rede-wendung)	*Das musst du mit eigenen Augen gesehen haben.*
You really can't be serious!	*Das kann doch nicht dein Ernst sein!*
you see	hier: *nämlich*
you should get going	*du musst los*
You took a real smack there.	*Da hast du einen heftigen Schlag abbe-kommen.*
You'd make a lovely couple.	*Ihr würdet ein hübsches Pärchen abgeben.*
you'd think	hier: *man könnte denken*
you're just imagining it	*das bildest du dir nur ein*
You've been promising me for the last three weeks that ...	*Du hast mir seit drei Wochen versprochen, dass ...*
You've got me mixed up.	*Du verwechselst mich.*
You've got nothing to worry about.	*Du brauchst keine Angst zu haben.*
You've got that funny look on your face again.	*Du guckst schon wieder so komisch.*
You've got to make sure you ...	*Du musst unbedingt ...*
You've got to suffer to be beautiful.	*Wer schön sein will, muss leiden.*

Kisses, Chaos and Dreams of Football

I - PSYCHOLOGY

1. Connect

Natalie's Freundin Mia will später Psychologin werden und hat sich schon so einiges an theoretischem Werkzeug angeeignet. Diese englischen Fachbegriffe, die sie dabei gelernt hat, kannst du mit ihren deutschen Übersetzungen verbinden.

1. negative energy	●	A Versuchskaninchen
2. frustration	●	B negative Energie
3. psychology	●	C klassische Symptome
4. guinea pig	●	D Frust
5. classic symptoms	●	E Psychologie

2. Odd one out

Als angehende Psychologin glaubt Mia, man sollte seinen Gefühlen freien Lauf lassen. Welcher dieser Gefühlsausbrüche passt hier nicht in die Reihe?

■ 1. to cry one's eyes out   ■ 2. to shout and yell loudly
■ 3. to burst out laughing   ■ 4. to stamp one's feet

Begründe deine Auswahl:

_____

> Konstruktionen mit „out"
> im Englischen haben oft
> ähnliche deutsche Über-
> setzungen mit „aus-" – z. B.
> to go **out** – *ausgehen*, sold
> **out** – *ausverkauft*.

3. Translation

Übersetze nun die Sätze 1. – 4. aus Aufgabe
2 ins Deutsche:

1. _____
2. _____
3. _____
4. _____

II - TWO-TIMING

4. Complete

„Two-timing" ist der Englische Begriff für Untreue in einer Beziehung:
Folgenden Sätzen zum Thema fehlt das Ende! Kannst du die zweite Hälfte
finden?

1. When she sits down with Mia in the garden, Natalie's heart is beating
   fast because...
   ■ A she is in love with Mia.
   ■ B she has had too many chocolate biscuits to eat.
   ■ C she is worried about what Mia is going to tell her.

2. In Leo's parents' shop, Natalie's heart starts beating faster again be-
   cause...
   ■ A she thinks he is on the phone to Vanessa.
   ■ B she thinks they are about to kiss.
   ■ C she drank too much coffee before going.

3. As Leo and Natalie are about to kiss, her heart starts beating faster because...
- ■ **A** she is excited about her new relationship with Leo.
- ■ **B** she had to run back to the youth centre after Mia called.
- ■ **C** she is still angry with Leo after the argument.

5. Fill in the gaps

In dem folgenden Text geht es darum, wie Felix Natalie betrogen hat. Leider sind ein paar Wörter zuviel hineingeraten. Fülle die Lücken mit jeweils passenden Wort aus der Box:

In this story, Mia shows Natalie **1.** _____ proof/suspicion/rumours

that Felix is cheating on her with Vanessa. Natalie doesn't want to believe

it, but the **2.** _____ danger/idea/evidence is overwhelming. So

Natalie makes up her mind to match Leo with Vanessa as

3. _____ reward/revenge/respect against Felix and decides to

confront him and get him to tell the **4.** _____ right/truth/lie.

Even when faced with Natalie and Vanessa at once, Felix is still a

5. _____ liar/layer/lair.

> Aufgepasst mit den Artikeln! Im Englischen sagt man immer „to tell **the** truth", dafür aber „to tell **a** lie".

6. Find the words

In dieser „falschen Schlange" sind einige Wörter zum Thema Treue und Untreue versteckt. Schreibe sie heraus.

Idatcheatgzdaxclloverattwotimeegprofhdsecretggreliespjeetrustfzgfadre

1. _____ 2. _____ 3. _____

4. _____ 5. _____ 6. _____

III – SELFISHNESS

7. True or false?

Natalie verhält sich in der Geschichte sehr selbstsüchtig: Sie setzt Leo als Werkzeug gegen Felix ein und denkt oft nur noch an sich. Diese Sätze beschreiben das Geschehen: Welche stimmen und welche sind falsch?

	TRUE	FALSE
1. Natalie sees Leo in the tram and wants him to say something nice.	▪	▪
2. Natalie asks Leo to steal Vanessa from Felix so that Felix will be angry.	▪	▪
3. Natalie changes her mind about eating ice-cream to avoid Felix.	▪	▪
4. Natalie realises that it is wrong to use Leo and apologises to him.	▪	▪

8. Anagram

Die Buchstaben in diesen Wörtern sind durcheinandergeraten.
Kannst du die wieder in Ordnung bringen?

1. fishselness   _____

2. goe   _____

3. sslethought   _____

4. ringcarun   _____

> Die englische Endung **-less** bei Adjektiven gleicht oft dem deutschen **-los** – z. B. shame**less** – scham**los**, remorse**less** – reue**los**.

9. Correct the text

Egoistischer als Natalie ist aber Felix. In diesem Text, der ihn beschreiben
soll, sind sechs Fehler hineingeraten. Streiche die Fehler durch und schreibe deine Verbesserung darüber.

Felix and Natalie are a couple, but Felix can't stay concentrated on Natalie.

He was caught on video kissing Victoria, who is a girl in the other class in

the year above. While Natalie is with him at his grandparents' shop he lies

to her about speaking to Victoria on the phone by telling Natalie it is his

aunt – but she is standing outside the shop at the time. When Natalie finds

him with Vanessa, he is very sorry about his behaviour.

IV – CHATTING UP GIRLS

10. Too many words!

Leo hat offenbar mehr Erfahrung mit Mädchen, als Natalie denkt. Er versteht es, mit ihr umzugehen.

> „To chat sb. up" heißt jemanden ansprechen, folglich gibt es viele sogenannte „chat-up lines" – oder „Anmachesprüche" zu Deutsch.

Diese Sätze, die seine Herangehensweise beschreiben, sind unvollständig – benutze Wörter aus dem untenstehenden Kasten, um die Lücken zu füllen. Achtung, nicht alle passen!

> lemonade   joke   jealous   upset   burger   ear
>
> angry   eye   laughing   polite   rude   shouting

1. Leo makes a _____ out of the fact that Natalie changes her mind.
2. Leo is able to keep _____-contact with Natalie while she looks at him.
3. Leo makes Natalie _____ by talking to Vanessa and _____ with her.
4. Leo is very _____ to Natalie – for example he buys her _____.

11. Connect the sentences

Diese Ratschläge von Natalie, wie Leo Vanessa ansprechen soll, sind durcheinandergeraten. Verbinde die Satzanfänge mit dem richtigen Ende.

1. All you've got to do is talk to her, although she...
___ A you straight away.

2. You've got make make the first move, then it...
___ B might react strangely at first.

3. If she looks you in the eyes, you've got to...
___ C look right back.

4. Don't be confused if she isn't nice to...
___ D will all be fine.

12. Crossword

Löse dieses Kreuzworträtsel! Fallen dir die Wörter nicht ein? Du findest sie in der Geschichte und den vorherigen Seiten.

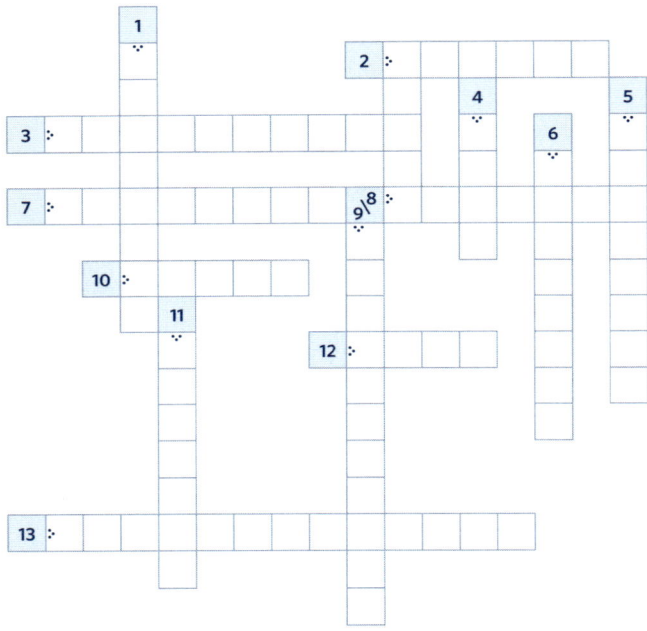

ACROSS

2 This can be used to film proof of cheating
3 This is used by boys to start talking to girls
7 Leo would like Natalie to play this sport
8 Another way of saying that you are cheating on your boyfriend
10 If you do this, people will find you attractive
12 This is where Natalie first talks to Leo
13 Players of this game could win dinner by candle light

DOWN

1 People often feel this emotion in relationships
2 This word could be used for Felix
4 This is a slang word for heavy kissing
5 Natalie wanted to eat one of these
6 Natalie wanted to play this
9 This is where young people meet
11 Leo's favourite method of transport

Kisses, Chaos and Rides on a Sledge

I - IDENTICAL TWINS

1. Connect

Marie und Hanna sind eineiige Zwillingsschwester. Kannst du diese englischen Begriffe zum Thema Zwillinge mit ihren deutschen Übersetzungen verbinden?

1. pregnancy   ●   A genetische Ähnlichkeit
2. genetic similarity   ●   B eineiige Zwillinge
3. offspring   ●   C Schwangerschaft
4. identical twins   ●   D zweieiige Zwillinge
5. non-identical twins ●   E Nachwuchs

> Wo im Deutschen ein
> Adjektiv vorneweg mit
> **nicht-** verneint wird,
> z. B. **nicht-**identisch,
> geschieht dies im
> Englischen meistens mit
> einem **non-**, **not** oder
> **no**, z. B. **non-**identical

2. Complete

In diesen Sätzen geht es um die Eigenschaften von Zwillingen. Suche das richtige Ende für jeden Satz:

1. Identical twins are identical because...
   - ■ A they wear the same clothes and have the same haircut.
   - ■ B they come from the same fertilised egg.
   - ■ C they have the same biological father.

2. Some parents of twins – like Hanna and Marie's mother – think it is a good idea to...
   - ■ A make sure the twins do everything together.
   - ■ B buy the same clothes for their twins.
   - ■ C send their twins to different schools.

3. Twins have very close relationships with each other because ...
   - ■ A they grow up with each other and have a special bond.
   - ■ B they are able to telepathically communicate with each other.
   - ■ C they are forced to by their parents.

3. Categorise

Schau dir die folgenden Wörter an. In welchen Dingen sind sich Marie und Hanna ähnlich – wo unterscheiden sie sich. Ordne die Wörter in die richtigen Spalten ein.

spontaneous   black hair   make-up   taste in boys   romantic

schoolfriends   relationship with Mrs Niederegger   voice

similar: different:

_____   _____

_____   _____

_____   _____

_____   _____

II – ILLNESS

4. Find the word

In diesem Durcheinander von Buchstaben sind Wörter über das Kranksein versteckt. Kannst du sie finden?

figuilllylvocoldwedbfeversickohllpainsfgahfbedrest

1. _____   2. _____

3. _____   4. _____

5. _____   6. _____

Im Englischen sind **ill** und **sick** fast deutungsgleich: „Are you ill?" oder „Are you sick?" bedeutet meistens dasselbe: „Bist du krank?". Manchmal kann **ill** aber auch „ärmlich" oder „bedürftig" bedeuten – „sick" bezieht sich dagegen immer aufs Kranksein.

5. Translate

Übersetze nun die Wörter von Aufgabe 4 ins Deutsche:

1. _____   2. _____   3. _____

4. _____   5. _____   6. _____

6. Odd one out

Die folgenden Vorschläge können dir bei Fieber, Grippe und Ähnlichem helfen. Was aber fällt hier aus der Reihe

- ▪ 1. Drink herbal tea with honey.
- ▪ 2. Wipe the forehead with a cold towel.
- ▪ 3. Take medicine such as painkillers.
- ▪ 4. Drink lots of water and stay in bed.

Wie unterscheidet sich dieser Vorschlag von den anderen?

_____

III - NOISY NEIGHBOURS

7. Fill in the gaps

In diesem Text geht es um die Nachbarin von Marie und Hanna, Frau Niederegger. Leider ist ihr Hund Lohengrin über einige Stellen gelaufen und hat ein paar Lücken Wörter verwischt. Wähle die passenden Wörter aus, die in diese Lücken passen:

Mrs Niederegger lives in the same block of 1. ⠿⠿⠿⠿⠿⠿ lego/flats/houses as

the girls and their mother. She owns a 2. ⠿⠿⠿⠿⠿⠿⠿⠿⠿⠿⠿ dachshund/

German shepherd/Great Dane dog called Lohengrin who is dressed in a small

doggy 3. ⠿⠿⠿⠿⠿⠿⠿⠿⠿⠿⠿ hat/scarf and gloves/jacket to protect him

against the cold. Mrs Niederegger likes the girls to

4. ⠿⠿⠿⠿⠿⠿⠿⠿⠿⠿⠿⠿⠿⠿⠿⠿⠿⠿⠿⠿⠿⠿

take her rubbish down/take the dog out/take a break

whenever they can. Even when the girls are ill

and in is cold outside, Mrs Niederegger has a

5. ⠿⠿⠿⠿⠿⠿⠿⠿⠿⠿⠿⠿⠿⠿⠿⠿⠿⠿⠿⠿⠿

packet of sweets/pile of letters for the post/long shopping list

for one of the twins to take care of.

> Das Englische hat viele
> Hundebezeichnungen
> aus dem Deutschen
> übernommen, z. B.
> **dachshund, sennen-**
> **hund** und **rotweiler**.
> Der **Deutsche**
> **Schäferhund**
> heißt **German**
> **shepherd**.

8. True or false?

Welche dieser Sätze über Frau Niederegger stimmen und welche nicht?

	TRUE	FALSE
1. Mrs Niederegger leaves the girls alone if they don't answer her shouts.	▪	▪
2. Mrs Niederegger tells Marie not to buy a certain type of sausage.	▪	▪
3. If the girls are loud in the evenings, Mrs Niederegger shouts at them.	▪	▪
4. Because she looks ill, Mrs Niederegger tells Marie not to go outside.	▪	▪

9. Complete the sentences

Diese Sätze beschreiben Momente in der Geschichte, in denen die Figuren laut sind. Leider sind die Anfänge und Enden durcheinandergeraten. Kannst du sie wieder richtig zusammenführen?

1. On the bus, the children are so loud   ___ A can not concentrate on her work.

2. When Mrs Niederegger wants something,   ___ B she shouts down the stairs.

3. Hanna moans so loudly that Marie   ___ C Mrs Niederegger asks for quiet.

4. When the twins talk to their boyfriends,   ___ D that Mrs. Schlotterbeck shouts.

IV – FUN IN THE SNOW

10. Too many words!

Im Schnee kann man jede Menge Spaß haben! Hier sind einige Wörter weggeschmolzen. Kannst du die passenden Wörter einsetzen, um die Sätze wieder zu vervollständigen? Aufgepasst: Es gibt mehr Wörter als Lücken!

> sledging   fur tree   snowballs   sledge   toboggan
>
> snowman   downhill   snowman   ice   run   ski piste

1. Throwing _____ can be very dangerous if they are too big or hard.

2. Tobogganing is another word for _____.

3. Building a _____ is something young children like to do.

4. If you take your sledge to a toboggan _____, you can go ride it _____ very fast.

Das Wort für **Schlitten** variiert, je nach dem, ob man in Großbritannien oder in den USA ist: Im Britischen Englisch heißt es **sledge**, im Amerikanischen schlicht **sled**.

11. Anagram

Die Buchstaben in diesen Wörtern sind durcheinandergeraten. Kannst du die wieder in Ordnung bringen?

1. gobognat nur _____

2. gslede _____

3. ternwi posrts yad _____

4. labnoslw _____

Kisses, Chaos and Dreams of Football

I – PSYCHOLOGY

1. Connect
1B, 2D, 3E, 4A, 5C

2. Odd one out
2, weil es eine positive Reaktion ist

3. Translate
sich die Augen ausheulen, laut schreien und brüllen, auflachen, mit den Füßen stampfen

II – TWO-TIMING

4. Complete
1C, 2A, 3A

5. Fill in the gaps
1. proof, 2. evidence, 3. revenge, 4. truth, 5. liar

6. Find the word
cheat, love-rat, two time, secret, lies, trust

III – SELFISHNESS

7. True or false
1. TRUE, 2. FALSE, 3. TRUE, 4. FALSE

8. Anagram
1. selfishness, 2. ego, 3. thoughtless, 4. uncaring

9. Correct the text
Felix and Natalie are a couple, but Felix can't stay concentrated on Natalie. He was caught on video kissing **Vanessa**, who is a girl in the other class **in their year**. While Natalie is with him at his **parents'** shop he lies to her about speaking to **Vanessa** on the phone by telling Natalie it is his **mum** – but she is standing outside the shop at the time. When Natalie finds him with Vanessa, he is **not** sorry about his behaviour.

10. Too many words!
1. joke, 2. eye, 3. jealous, laughing, 4. polite, lemonade

11. Connect the sentences
1B, 2D, 3C, 4A

12. Crossword
Across
2. camera
3. chat-up line
7. football
8. two-time
10. smile
12. tram
13. table-football

Down
1. jealousy
2. cheat
4. snog
5. ice-cream
6. mini-golf
9. youth centre
11. bicycle

LOVE-QUESTIONS

So könnten Deine Antworten aussehen. Im SMS-Glossar findest du viele Abkürzungen, wie man sie in SMS verwendet.

```
1. Hey Mia! I sat next 2
   Leo on the tram and told
   him Vanessa loved him!
   That will teach Felix!
```

Natalie hat Leo erzählt, dass Vanessa auf ihn steht. Sie ist gekränkt und will Leo und Vanessa verkuppeln, um Felix eine Lektion zu erteilen.

```
2. Hi Mia! I was just with
   Felix — that guy's such
   a liar! Now waiting at
   football practice 4 Leo.
   Gonna be on the team ;-)
```

Natalie war gerade mit Felix unterwegs und er hat sie belogen: Als Vanessa angerufen hat, hat er Natalie erzählt, seine Mutter sei am Telefon – die stand aber leider in guter Sichtweite Natalies – ohne Telefon!

```
3. Hey Mi-baby! Football
   practice was cancelled.
   Now on back of Leo's
   bike and going 2 get an
   ice-cream! Yum yum!
```

Das Fußballtraining ist ausgefallen, also hat Natalie Leo vorgeschlagen, dass sie jetzt ein Eis essen gehen. In der Eisdiele will sie mit ihm über Vanessa reden...

```
4. Yes, I'll be there in a
   sec! And in the end we
   didn't get ice-cream —
   we're at the minigolf-
   course instead! X
```

Natalie hat gemerkt, dass die Eisdiele gefährlich nah an der Martinstraße liegt, wo Felix' Eltern ihren Laden haben. Sie will nicht, dass er sie mit Leo sieht. Daher schlägt sie eine Runde Minigolf vor.

```
5. Hi Mia! Just broke up
   with Felix + Vanessa
   broke up with him 2! He
   lied 2 us both!
```

Natalie hat Felix mit Vanessa erwischt. Als sie Schluss mit ihm macht, erzählt sie Vanessa warum und diese macht es ihr gleich nach.

Kisses, Chaos and Rides on a Sledge ♥

··

I - IDENTICAL TWINS

1. Connect
1C, 2A, 3E, 4B, 5D

2. Complete
1B, 2C, 3A

3. Categorise
similar: black hair, taste in boys, relationship with Mrs Niederegger, voice
different: spontaneous, make-up, romantic, school-friends

··

II - ILLNESS

4. Find the word
ill, cold, fever, sick, pain, bed rest

5. Translate
1. krank, 2. kalt, Erkältung, 3 - Fieber, 4 - krank, 5 - Schmerzen, 6 - Bettruhe

6. Odd one out
3, because medicine is not a natural remedy – *Arzneimittel wie Schmerztabletten sind kein Naturheilmittel.*

··

III - NOISY NEIGHBOURS

7. Fill in the gaps
1. flats, 2. dachshund, 3. jacket, 4. take the dog out, 5. long shopping list

8. True or false
1. FALSE, 2. TRUE, 3. TRUE, 4. FALSE

9. Complete the sentences
1D, 2B, 3A , 4C

10. Too many words!
1. snowballs, 2. sledging, 3. snowman, 4. run, downhill

11. Anagram
1. toboggan run, 2. sledge, 3. winter sports day, 4. snowball

LOVE-QUESTIONS

1. Hey! I had 2 go shopping
   4 Mrs Niederegger. I'm
   at the butchers talking
   to Andys sister. I might
   go for you... :-)

*Marie musste für Frau Niederegger einkaufen und steht jetzt beim Metzger und unter-
hält sich mit Andys Schwester. Dadurch erfährt sie, dass Andy auch beim Wintersporttag dabei ist, weshalb sie sich doch dafür entscheidet, ihre Schwester beim Sporttag zu
vertreten.*

2. Hey sis! Thanks 4
   breakfast but I wasn't
   hungry. Made the bus +
   people think I'm u, it's
   working! :-)

*Marie hatte keinen Hunger und hat sich deswegen nicht an den liebevoll von Hanna
gedeckten Frühstückstisch gesetzt. Ihre Doppelgänger-Strategie geht aber augenscheinlich auf.*

3. Hey Hanna! Mrs Schlot-
   terbeck kept all our
   phones while we were
   sledging. On the way
   home now. xxx

*Da Frau Schlotterbeck alle Handys eingesammelt hat, konnte Marie Hannas Anrufe
nicht beantworten.*

4. Hi mum! Not feeling very
   well. Hanna is better
   than yesterday. We've
   both been in bed … C u
   l8ter! xxx

Marie geht es nicht gut, weil sie erschöpft und verletzt ist. Dabei kann sie aber ihrer Mutter nicht erzählen, dass sie auf dem Sporttag war, weil die beiden Schwestern ja zu Hause bleiben sollten. Dass es Hanna, die gerade draußen war, offensichtlich besser geht, kann aber natürlich erzählt werden.

5. Yes!!!!!!!!!

Manchmal reicht eine Ein-Wort-Antwort. Vor allem, wenn die Zeit nicht reicht, um mehr zu schreiben, weil man anderweitig beschäftigt ist …

Freches Englisch mit den Frechen Mädchen

Hier dreht sich alles um die kleinen Missverständnisse zwischen Jungs und Mädchen, die Tücken der Pubertät und den ganz alltäglichen Wahnsinn mit Eltern, Geschwistern und Freundinnen.
So könnt Ihr mit den frechen Büchern ganz nebenbei Euren englischen Wortschatz erweitern und Eure Grammatikkenntnisse verbessern. Alle Lovestorys auch zum Anhören auf MP3-CD.

Alle Bände aus einer Reihe:

Kisses, Cuddles & Holiday Love
ISBN: 978-3-12-010022-5

Love, Twists & Blissful Kisses
ISBN: 978-3-12-010023-2

Flirting, Fun & Chaotic Kisses
ISBN: 978-3-12-010021-8

www.pons.de